BOMBS ON
BRAMALL LANE

BY KEN LEARY

★ACM RETRO

Published by ACM Retro Ltd,
The Grange,
Church Street,
Dronfield,
Sheffield S18 1QB.

Visit ACM Retro at:
www.acmretro.com

BOMBS OVER
BRAMALL LANE

For Doris

Contents

Foreword

Much has been said about the ordeal of the Sheffield adult population in World War Two.

The sacrifices of the local men who went overseas to fight have been well documented and the courageous work of the women who took their places in Sheffield's munitions factories was finally recognised by Prime Minister, Gordon Brown, in 2010.

Their wartime experiences regularly scarred them for life (both physically and mentally) and it would take the birth of a whole new generation to finally start to shake off the dark shadow of the rise and fall of the Third Reich.

But what of the children whose formative years were spent growing up against the backdrop of air raids, the horrors of the Sheffield Blitz and growing up amongst the bombsites?

How did they remember the madness enveloping their lives – madness that would have seemed perfectly normal as they'd never known anything else?

Ken Leary, sadly, never lived to see his memoir being published. His son Kevin said "he would have been choked to think others would have taken even the slightest interest in his life".

'Bombs Over Bramall Lane' opens a forgotten window on a forgotten world.

You only have to read the first few lines to appreciate what kind of a world it was for a child.

Whilst the city celebrated at the news of war finally coming to an end after six tortuous years Ken, like many other children, felt a tinge of disappointment because "the game had finally ended".

His vivid recollections of wandering through the ruins of the city centre in the immediate aftermath of the first night of the Sheffield Blitz of December 1940 are pin sharp – the devastation, the acrid smells and an insight into the coping mechanisms of a young child witnessing the destruction of much of everything he has ever known.

As families struggle to cope with 21th century recession, the worst since the 1930s if analysts are to be believed, Ken Leary's story proves children can get by quite happily without a king's ransom spent on material goods.

Sailing a piece of wood in the bombed out crater that used to be Atkinsons department store was fun enough for a child who'd never known anything else. In fact much of Ken's childhood was spent happily playing in the ruins of The Moor which was totally flattened.

Despite living through years of post war austerity and hardship, Ken Leary actually preferred his war experiences to the financial woes of the 21st century. He signs off at the end of his book with a quote he overheard from two old women at a bus stop who were discussing the state of the economy: "I'll tell you what, I'm bloody glad I'm going instead of coming aren't you." The other woman was in full agreement Ken said. I'm pretty sure Ken Leary was too.

Neil Anderson, author of 'Sheffield's Date With Hitler'

Introduction

This book was written, I feel sure, because my father knew that he had one last journey to make. There was no getting away from it and that was that. He was a methodical man in many respects, but he was also a great beginner, and not always a great finisher of the jobs that he started. This was different. He had to get his house in order (quite literally) and I think that he also wanted to leave behind some living memento, particularly for his younger grandchildren to remember him by.

His thoughts therefore turned to his own childhood nearly seventy years before – now what a story that would make. A happy childhood certainly, but hardly an idyllic one; money was scarce, luxuries few and of course there was the small matter of dodging the bombs being dropped by Hitler's Luftwaffe. Thanks to them Sheffield was torn apart, but when the new city arose from the ashes, people's lives and attitudes had changed forever. Don't get me wrong, my father fully appreciated all the benefits of the Nuclear-age, and all the mysteries of the microchip - but has the price been too high? Are we under too many pressures and has childhood lost too much of its innocence? This book looks back to an era and a way of life that few would recognise today. It is a modest and light-hearted glimpse of ordinary life in the inner-city during the 1940s where, despite all the horrors of war, the hardships and adversity, there was hope and optimism by the bucketful; and for the kids in particular, given just a little imagination - life could still be what you wanted it to be.

For those of us not around at the time, the war years tend to be visualised in shades of black and white because of the newsreels and other monochrome images with which we are familiar. This somehow reflects the mood of the times, but of course it is a gross distortion. There was light and colour also and from a child's perspective the summers were always warm and seemingly endless - hence my father's original working title: 'Did the Sun Always Shine?' The cycle of life carried on and Hitler was not going to be allowed to spoil things. For the Hereford Street gang, apart from the usual street-games, football and bike-rides - there was bomb-site salvage (just one of many schemes for making a few extra coppers), mummering at Christmas (what?) and rambles deep into the Derbyshire countryside – not exactly 'The Darling Buds of May' but something of that spirit.

If there is any theme running through this book, it is a very simple one; that despite the fires of war and the gloom of post war austerity there was still fun to be had. Very often this cost no more than the price of a tram-ticket

8

- although the purchase of a 'Wiggie's gas-pipe' bicycle (price £18) did place a greater strain on the imagination. For older readers there is much here that will be familiar. For the rest of us, if we can tear ourselves away from our flat-screens, Blackberries and MP3s, and perhaps give just a little pause for thought - it is a fascinating window into the past.

Kevin Leary

Chapter One

PICTURES IN THE MIND

Even now after all these years I can still recall the moment quite clearly: 'Waar's o'er. Waar's o'er.'

The words spilled excitedly from the lips of one of our friends as he dashed round the corner from Hereford Street to inform us (in a typical Sheffield accent) that the war had finally come to an end.

At that historic moment in time, as I remember it, a group of us were having a contest to see who could shin-up a Belisha beacon the quickest. The Belisha beacon was one of two that stood at the bottom of Bramall Lane, at the junction with Hereford Street; the date was 8th May 1945. I was nearly nine years old at the time but in a strange way, instead of being elated as we should have been after hearing this tremendous news, I definitely remember feeling a little bit disappointed. It felt as though the game had finally ended just when we were winning; because to us kids the last six years had been, in our minds at least, one long adventure game. It was us against the Germans. Those thoughts, plus the sights and sounds of war, had dominated our young lives for so long and the memories that were imprinted on our minds would last a lifetime. Of course, being children, the darker side of the war never entered our tiny minds. The misery, the destruction, the killing and all the heart-ache attached to it; all that side of war, belonged to the adults. So it came as no surprise really to see the grown-ups celebrating the news with great enthusiasm. I can recall one incident that happened later that same evening concerning my own mother, who as far as I knew at the time, wasn't a drinker by any means. She was invited to have a celebratory glass with some of the neighbours in the local pub, the *Chantrey Arms* which stood at the bottom of Bramall Lane just round the corner from our house. Sometime before closing time, which was ten o'clock in those days, mother had to be helped home by two ladies, one on either side supporting her. It appeared she'd had one or two 'shandys' too many. They ushered her indoors, with me following behind, and as they were helping her upstairs to bed I heard her utter those immortal words:

'Never again! Never again!'

And for the rest of her life - she never did.

But she had probably enjoyed herself more in those few hours than she had done at anytime during the previous six years. She had certainly earned and deserved it - and so had everyone else.

I was born on Friday 17ᵗʰ July 1936, starting life in the bedroom of a terraced house in Attercliffe Sheffield, at number 7 Twelve O'clock Street to be precise. This rented property belonged to my grandfather on my father's side (the house is now long demolished). I lived there with my parents Bill and Louisa and my elder sister Joan for about the first three years of my life, but I have absolutely no memories of this early period at all. Then just after the start of the Second World War, in late nineteen thirty nine or early nineteen forty, we moved across the city to a new address; number 58 Hereford Street, close to the bottom of Bramall Lane. This rented property had originally belonged to my mother's parents, who, much to my grandmother's disgust, had moved from an excellent abode in Millhouses so that my grandfather, who was the organist at the Victoria Hall in Norfolk Street, could easily walk there. It was after they had both passed away that my parents took over the tenancy. This house was to be my spiritual home for more than a decade of my early life, a home packed with so many happy childhood memories, and a few not so happy.

It was the beginning of a childhood so different from anything today, and in a country so unrecognisable from the Britain of the present time. Even the climate was different. The summers were sunny, warm and long. In winter sledging and snowball fights were always on the menu - with no health and safety jobsworths poking their noses in.

Hereford Street at that period was in two parts. The top half ran from close to the bottom of The Moor, where the Manpower building now stands, down to the bottom of Bramall Lane which then extended much further than it does today. The bottom half then continued from Bramall Lane to the junction with St Mary's Road (now St Mary's Gate), and the top half consisted mainly of small old-fashioned shops on either side of the road, plus a couple of pubs, the *Hereford Arms* and the *Bridge Inn*.

Of the shops, the one I remember with the most affection was *Shaws Bread Shop* with that gorgeous smell of fresh-baked bread as you entered the door. An errand to this shop also had its perks and on the way home I'd nibble off the corners of the loaf which always got me an ear-bashing from my mother. The other thing I remember vividly for some unknown reason was the price of a large loaf, tuppence three farthings, plus the fact that it seemed to stay at that price forever.

Another shop I remember well was *Thomas's* horse-meat shop. It was to this shop that my mother used to send me for two penny worth of lights for our cat Sandy, appropriately a large ginger tom. To this day I'm still not sure what exactly lights are. I know what they looked like. The best way to describe them would be to imagine the butcher cutting the insides out of an animal, (obviously a horse in this case) smashing it into pulp with a mallet, slapping it into a newspaper, wrapping it up and then handing it over the counter. By the time I'd dashed home with it my hands would be covered in blood which had seeped through the newspaper; there were obviously no perks with this errand!

Other shops also come to mind. A hardware shop which had that peculiar aroma of paraffin which all old-fashioned hardware shops seemed to have in those days, and *FitzPatricks* the green-grocers shop where a group of us one day (just after the end of the war), stood gazing through the window in amazement at our first sighting of a banana. We'd heard of them of course and finally we could now see one with our own eyes, but it would still be a long time before we actually got our lips around one.

Of the other shops that I can recall was a haberdashery shop, a newsagents (were I had my first ever job as a paper boy at ten shillings a week), a butchers shop whose name I can't remember, and a café whose name I can remember - *Speechleys*. At the very top, on the corner adjoining The Moor, was the *New Era* furniture shop. So that was the top half of Hereford Street, of which incidentally a small portion still remains to this day, but alas none of the shops.

The bottom half of Hereford Street was the residential part. It commenced at the junction of Bramall Lane and ended at the junction with St Mary's Road. On the left-hand side of the street stood a factory which was busy and bustling in its heyday. I well recall the sound of the factory hooters blasting-off to signal dinner breaks and knocking-off time, and the workforce pouring through the gates making their way home. Occasionally a crowd would gather outside the gates all staring at something on the ground. It would be old Harry the paper man having one of his regular epileptic fits. Every day for as long as I remember; hail, rain, snow or blow - Harry would be there outside the gates selling *The Star*.

On the opposite side of the road stood the houses, all built before the turn of the century in Victorian times. Blocks of terraced-type dwellings, the majority back to back, and incorporated into the terrace were a small grocery shop, a sweet shop, a funeral parlour and a pub - the *Bricklayer's Arms* slap-bang in the middle. The terrace continued around the corner and up Bramall Lane as far as St Mary's Road and a lane bisected part of it. Our abode, number 58 was four doors above the pub which was an alcoholics dream residence and a popular venue for nightly street entertainment by people singing their way home after a good night out. It was a regular occurrence in those days after the war had ended, but alas not anymore. Maybe people today have nothing to sing about, or is the beer brewed differently from yesteryear - too many chemicals instead of the natural ingredients. Oh yes, the beer in those days was definitely singing beer!

Our house was typical of all the hundreds of other terraced- type houses in the city and in today's estate-agents lingo the spec would read: 'a desirable residence, within easy reach of the town centre, a two bedroom dwelling consisting of a dining/living room with single aspect, benefiting from a small kitchen, one first floor bedroom, with an attic bedroom and a coal-cellar/storage area'.

My domain, from moving in to moving out, was the attic. The bedroom belonged to my mother and sister because my father by this time had made alternative arrangements. He had volunteered to join the RAF and gone off to fight Hitler, or so he told us. My mother thought it a bit strange because twenty five years earlier (at the age of sixteen), he had volunteered to join the army and went to France to fight the Kaiser's army, now here he was once again volunteering. What was it with my father? Did he dislike Germans that much he wanted to fight them twice? Perhaps he just liked uniforms, or maybe he was just simply trying to get out of decorating the new house.

Our house must have been one of the better properties. We had a separate kitchen, the size of a postage stamp, but a separate kitchen nonetheless, with a door separating it from the living room. In nearly all of the other houses the kitchen sink was in the living room between the chimney breast and the front window. In our kitchen we had all the modern conveniences of the day; a single gas ring, a large shallow brown stone sink with a tap and running cold water, plus hot running water when the kettle had boiled. There was also a small built-in copper with a fire-place underneath for heating up large quantities of water, used either for the washing of clothes, or filling the tin bath on bath night which in our household was on Friday night. When I became a little older I was given the job of chief bath-emptier; the reason given for my promotion was that, being the scruffiest, this entitled me to be the last in the bath-water when everyone else had used it and had gone to bed. Whilst the first person was taking a bath, the rest of us formed an orderly queue upstairs awaiting our turn.

There was a small window in the kitchen which offered excellent views across the back-yard to the outside toilet-blocks. That was after they had knocked down the air-raid shelter that had stood in the middle of the yard after the war ended. The only heating in the house was in the living room and came from the fire-place in the old Yorkshire cooking range, a masterpiece of cooking equipment for the Victorian housewife. Once a week mother would 'black-lead' it until it shone like ebony. Sitting in front of this on a cold winter's night, it was the only warm spot in the whole house - apart from being tucked up in bed. It was in the oven of this range that my mother did practically all her cooking, the same as every body else had to. Later on, after the war was over, she modernised and acquired a double gas ring. This meant she could now have two cooking utensils on the go at the same time instead of having one balancing dangerously on the fire.

Something has always puzzled me about these old Yorkshire ranges. Lots of women at that time of day, including my own mother, used to bake some of their own bread. They were baked in the oven and called flat oven-bottom cakes. When ready they would be taken outside and placed on the window-sill on a piece of newspaper. What was all that about? Did all the soot filling the air at that time make them taste better?

Another use for the oven in winter was to heat up the bed warmer. This was a large ceramic object filled with sand. After a while in the oven, when the sand had heated up, it was wrapped in a piece of blanket and then placed in the bed an hour or so before bedtime. The oven plate, which was a removable metal shelf in the oven, was also wrapped up and placed in the bed. This made bedtime in winter a little more pleasant. Apart from the coal for the fire, the cellar also stored my mother's washing day equipment; the galvanised washtub, the rubbing board, the 'posher' (the what?) and later on her pride and joy - the latest *Acme* wringing machine. This had adjustable rubber rollers which she clamped to a portable galvanised metal frame - the wringer being hand operated of course. Previous to this she had used the old mangle in the cellar and whoever got this down the cellar steps must have finished up with a double-hernia. On washing day all this paraphernalia had to be brought up from the cellar into the living room and then returned again after the washing was finished.

One thing that has always amused me is that well-meaning saying that old people occasionally come out with: 'when we were young - people could leave their doors open', which was quite true to a certain extent. But why did everybody have a chain on their cellar-grates? Was it to stop people stealing the coal, or from stealing the cellar-grate for scrap. I presume it was to protect the coal which was rationed like everything else during the war. I remember that when the coalman came to our house to deliver coal, on my mother's instructions I had to stand at the bottom of the cellar steps and count how many bags were thrown down the grate just to make sure she got what she paid for - and also that she had received her full allowance. On a shelf by the coal-chute stood the penny-in-the-slot gas meter. Yes, believe it or not, one old penny. Why I should remember this for over sixty years is beyond me - unless it was the novelty putting the penny in the slot like some fairground fruit-machine. Incidentally, when it was emptied by the gas man, a rebate of a few shillings was always returned.

On the right at the bottom of the cellar steps was a stone table used for various tasks and storage, but mainly for any perishable food. There were no household fridges in those days. As a precaution, because of the approaching war, builders had been into each cellar and had knocked out small openings to link up all the adjacent neighbouring cellars. These had then been fitted a small door frame with a breakable asbestos door. The idea being that if the house was bombed while the occupants where sheltering down in the cellar, and they had been lucky enough to survive, they could smash through the door and escape into the cellar next door. All the house-cellars in the block were joined by this escape route.

It was shortly after moving into this house that my first childhood memories start to manifest themselves, but only as pictures in the mind of a child. Actual day by day content is obviously none existent, as is the order in which the events took place. One of the first images that jumps into my mind is the flooding of the living room. It must have been one washing day as I recall the wash tub, half full of water, standing there in front of the kitchen door. It was tilted at a slight angle resting on a small stool ready for emptying with the ladling can. I remember trying to look inside when suddenly it rolled off the stool, and then it is lying on its side with the contents disappearing under the kitchen table and side-board, and soaking our new pegged rug which was rolled up under the table. I can hear my mother now - shouting and panicking at the same time as I shot through the front door.

I remember another incident with the words:

'Don't you go on that road with that bike.'

It must have been one of the first 'don't do's' that I ever heard from my mother – but then again probably not, the first will have been:

'Don't you ever go near that wash tub again.'

On this particular occasion it concerned my three-wheeled bike which I'd learned to ride in the back-yard. I obviously couldn't wait to broaden my horizons so the next step was to take it on the pavement outside our house, and then up and down the street. Gradually I was taking bigger liberties, as kids often do, going that yard or two further, like disappearing around the corner and along the bottom of Bramall Lane (the part that no longer exists). After getting away with that, and with no ear-bashing, I took liberties to the extreme with a trip round the entire block. Even now after all these years I can still recall the thrill of childhood adventure that was in my mind as I peddled along Bramhall Lane; past the *Chantrey* pub and on to the *Norfolk Arms,* a left turn down St

Mary's Road (now St Mary's Gate), another left turn, back up Hereford Street and home. All this was on the pavement of course - adventurous stuff for a young child of about four years old. Imagine parents letting kids do anything like that in this day and age. But things were a lot different back then; traffic was extremely sparse and you'd probably have had more chance of being knocked over by a horse and cart than a motor vehicle. This, I imagine was what prompted my future interest in what lay beyond the next horizon, and my eventual enthusiasm for the countryside and travel. But it would be many years before I got my bum on another bike- saddle.

Denby Street nursery was just off Bramall Lane, as it still is nearly seventy years later, and it was within these walls I had my first introduction to school life. Two incidents are ingrained in my memory of this school. The first concerns the underground air-raid shelter in the playground and the methods that were used to entice us down the steps and into the gloomy interior. We were usually bribed with sweets. When the sirens sounded, the children who went in under their own steam were rewarded with a sweet, whilst the others were carried in kicking and screaming until they got used to the regular ritual. I remember taking the first option. The second image was what I called the sleeping lesson. Oh yes, we were all expected to lie down on oval-shaped mats, sometimes outdoors if the weather was warm, and drop off into dreamland for an hour or so like good little boys and girls - a fat lot of chance!

It was during this period in my young life that I was introduced to the horrors of war by a journey, partly through the city centre, that I took with my mother and sister. A journey that is still etched in my mind even though I was only just turned four years old at the time. It was the morning after the night of the first Sheffield blitz. Bombs had dropped all around us, many properties had been destroyed and people killed. As we came out of our house the first thing I remember seeing was a white enamelled soap dish lying on the pavement, surrounded with broken glass, in front of our next door neighbour's shattered living room window. This was one of the houses with its sink by the side of the living room window and the soap dish had probably been on the window-bottom. Recalling this incident many years later, it occurred to me that if a bomb-blast had been the cause, the glass should have been blown inside the house. But according to someone more knowledgeable about these matters, a blast occurring many yards away could in fact suck the glass out. A direct hit on an air-raid shelter on Porter Street, which was just round the corner from us, had claimed many lives and this could have been the cause.

My mother's usual route was to walk down to the bottom of St Mary's Road, then up Granville Road to City Road. But St Mary's Road was blocked off because of an unexploded landmine, so we found ourselves walking up Arundel Street which ran parallel with The Moor. It was here that the sights of war first met my eyes. The air was filled with smoke and the acrid smell of burning buildings, a smell that has lingered in my memory for all these years. Grey canvas hose-pipes, with brass fittings that coupled them together, criss-crossed the road shooting off in various directions. I recall jumping over them like it was a game we were playing. Some game!

As we carried on up the road towards the Graves Building, water was streaming down the gutters towards us, leaking from the hose-pipes. Suddenly we were in front of the Graves Art Gallery and it is here the memory and the incident ends - what happened after that is a complete blank. My sister, six years older than me, recalls the event differently which is probably nearer to what took place. This is her account. The morning after the night of the first Sheffield blitz, even though our house was still standing, my mother didn't want to stay there; she was too nervous, fearing the Luftwaffe may return. She suggested that we go to her sisters who lived on the Manor estate away from the city centre. She planned a route we could walk; it took us down Hereford Street, then a left turn into St Mary's Road - but on turning it was quite a shock to see a row of bay-windowed houses on the right-hand side completely demolished. In the middle of the road was a huge crater caused by a landmine and all the occupants of the houses had been killed.

We turned back into Hereford Street, then right at the bottom of Bramall Lane into Porter Street which ran parallel to The Moor. An underground shelter had taken a direct hit and as we passed, bodies were being brought out. We were then diverted to a lane that led to Moorhead (this is what I probably mistook later for Arundel Street). We continued on down Fargate and High Street, past Walsh's department store which was still smoking and opposite which there was a burnt-out tram. We passed the Marples Hotel in Fitzalan Square, which had also received a direct hit killing many of the customers, and then crossed over to Commercial Street. From there the journey continued up Duke Street and City Road to Manor Top, then a left turn on to Prince of Wales Road followed by a right-turn up Ravencarr Road, and finally on to Stanground Road where my aunt lived. We arrived on the Friday morning and stayed there for over a week, but on the following Sunday the bombers returned, this time targeting the east end. As we dashed down the garden to my aunt's Anderson shelter incendiary bombs were dropping all around us.

I was now to enter a period of my young life that I shall never forget. The majority of the events that occurred are still blurred pictures in my mind, and the actual details of day to day happenings and the order in which they

Me with mum on
Hereford Street

The view from our front
door looking towards
the top half of Hereford
Street, with the Bridge
pub partly hidden by the
bus

occurred are extremely vague. The downward spiral started one day when I opened the cellar door. For some unknown childish reason, I was leaning over, peering down into the gloomy cellar below and suddenly I lost my grip on the door-jamb and plunged head first down the cellar steps. As luck would have it I missed the edge of the stone steps with my head and took the brunt of the fall with the shoulder and I finished up in the Royal Hospital on West Street (long since demolished) being treated for a broken collar bone.

As if that wasn't enough, a little later while strutting about strapped up, I tripped over the fender surrounding the fire in our living room and fell on to the fire-grate burning the fingers on the other hand. Things were now beginning to hot up in more ways than one. I recovered from these accidents, but fate hadn't finished with me yet and had more sinister plans in store for me - plans that would very nearly cost me my life.

The war had now begun in earnest. The Battle of Britain had almost been won in the skies over southern England, but suddenly the Germans altered their tactics and it was now the turn of the civilian population. The sirens were now sounding on a regular basis, sometimes two and three times during the night, although most of the time they were false alarms. I recall very often being woken by my mother and taken from my warm bed down into the cold damp cellar. Mother never used the air-raid shelter up in the yard preferring to take her chance in the cellar like lots of other people. Being woken up and transferred to the cellar was now happening quite regularly, and although I was probably wrapped in warm blankets whilst in the cellar, the change from warm to cold finally took its toll. I developed bronchial pneumonia and was now seriously ill - it would be well over a year before I finally recovered. I remember very little of the early months of the illness, my bed was brought down from the attic and placed under the living room window. This made it easier for my mother to care for me, and for the doctors to treat me. I don't know if I was hospitalised initially or not and I can't even remember it being mentioned in later years. What I do know however is that I was laid up in that bed for a long time; that long that when I finally emerged I had to learn to walk all over again. Apparently at one period I was so ill (so I was told years later) that the doctors informed my mother that it was very doubtful I would survive. But my mother was having none of that and with her loving care, and a guardian angel, we proved the doctor's wrong.

After many months in bed I slowly started to improve. It was a long process, but I gradually started to get stronger and more alert and it was now that the pictures start to re-appear in my mind once again. I remember people coming into the house and staring at me lying in bed, probably fondling rosaries as though they had just witnessed a miracle, ha-ha! Some, very kindly brought presents. I remember one present distinctly. It was a book about the south-sea islands with pictures of black-faced children playing on a beach under palm trees. Mrs Gilvray, who owned the chip shop at the bottom of Bramall Lane, brought me some lead soldiers. Someone else brought a model of an army tank, made of wood, which was also a money box.

It was during this same period, when I was laid up, that my only claim to fame occurred (so I was told later - not being able to recall the event myself). Winston Churchill actually waved to me personally; well he raised his hand and gave his famous two fingered gesture in my direction, so I can only hope he meant it as a friendly gesture.

It came about during his visit to Sheffield in order to inspect the bomb damage[1]. Our area had had its fair share of damage with bombs dropping all around us, one in particular within yards of our house. This one hit an air-raid shelter on Porter Street killing quite a few people, whilst others fell on shops bordering The Moor. One fell on the Bramall Lane stand of Sheffield United Football Club, and a further one or two fell on a row of terraced houses round the corner on St Mary's Road - again killing most of the occupants. Another bomb, probably from the same aircraft, hit Duchess Road School at the corner of Shoreham Street. It was probably as a result of these actions that Mr Churchill found himself being driven up Hereford Street at the same moment in time as I was kneeling up in bed, with my head under the curtain peering out through the window. He apparently spotted me and gave a wave.

As the days and weeks passed my health improved and I once again re-entered the world of the living. The next landmark I remember was learning to walk. Because I had been laid up in bed for so long, the muscles in my legs had deteriorated slightly making it almost impossible to walk. Having to hold on to someone's hand and trying to walk across the living room with my legs going in all directions, is something I shall never forget. But after persevering I gradually got the hang of it again and it wasn't long before I could walk across the living room on my own - from the bed to the step at the bottom of the bedroom stairs. Gradually the strength started to return to my legs and I could now move about more easily. I was now able to climb the stairs once again, so the bed was returned to the attic and me with it. This must have been a big relief all round, especially for my mother because the trauma of the sirens and the bombs were challenging enough to the nervous system without having a child with a life-threatening illness to care for. Then, on top of all that, there would

---

[1] The Prime Minister's visit to Sheffield took place on 8th November 1941. He inspected the bomb damage in the city centre including that on the Moor (explaining his presence on Hereford Street), visited a shell factory in the east-end and also waved to crowds from the balcony of the Town Hall.

have been the problem of her paying the doctor's bills as there was no National Health Service in those days.

It was shortly after this period, as my health continued to improve, that my father came home for a spell of leave. At this time he was stationed in South Wales, close by the village of Nash near Newport. Adjacent to the RAF camp where he was based was a farm owned by Mr and Mrs Perry with whom he had become friendly, and during conversation he must have mentioned my recent illness. They very kindly invited him to bring me down to stay on the farm with them and their family. Looking back now, apart from giving me the opportunity to reap the benefits of living on a farm in the country, it would also have given my mother a well deserved break. My older sister Joan had already been evacuated to a stately-home near Southwell in Nottinghamshire, so I now found myself on a crowded train heading towards some unknown destination.

I remember nothing of the journey and the first image in my mind is of walking up a country lane with the daylight fading, then entering what turned out to be the farmhouse. The first thing I remember is a large roaring fire, but apart from that the room appeared to be dimly lit. There were people sat round a table looking at me and I remember not feeling very happy in this new environment. After a while my father left and I was now on my own. Funnily enough, this didn't bother me at first; perhaps it was because I hardly knew him due to the circumstances we were living under during wartime. The next thing I remember was standing in front of the fire and being undressed for bed by a lady I had just clapped eyes on - and this is when the tears started to flow. I have absolutely no recollections of going to bed that night, or any other night, but I know I soon lost my shyness and quickly got used to my new life on the farm with the Perry family. Like I have said previously, all my memories, especially those of my time spent on the farm, are fleeting images etched in my mind, but in what order they occurred I have no idea. For instance, I remember being in some type of barn or dairy and drinking milk from a glass, but I don't ever recall seeing any cows.

One incident that really sticks out in my mind happened one day when I was following Mr Perry, (apparently I used to follow him about like a lapdog). We had crossed a couple of large fields and had then come to a dyke, which we crossed by a narrow wooden plank bridge, and were faced with a high sloping bank. Mr Perry climbed to the top and I scrambled up after him, but I was quite unprepared for the view that hit me. There in front of us were miles of open sea under an endless sky, with the waves lapping onto the beach at the bottom of the bank that we were stood upon. It physically took my breath away. The sudden impact, without any warning, of the complete contrast between enclosed fields and a vision of miles of open sea left me stunned. Even the sight of the lighthouse hadn't given me any clue or warning, having never before seen a lighthouse or known what one was. But I remember, every time I went up that bank after that, I would crawl up on my hands and knees, and gradually peer over the top, absorbing the view a little at a time.

Another vision still fresh in my mind is that of feeding the chickens with what I can now presume was corn from a bucket; throwing it all over the yard and watching the chicken's zero in on it from all directions - then going with Mrs Perry to collect eggs from the chicken hut. The hut was in the corner of a field away from the house and attached to one side of the hut was a row of nesting boxes with a long narrow door, which when dropped open, revealed the backs of the hens sat on their nests. What makes this incident stick in my memory is probably the method that I used to get at the eggs. Mrs Perry would put her hand gently under the sitting hen and take out all the eggs, but there was no way I would dare do that. My method was to poke the hen off the nest with a stick and then collect the eggs - it never failed.

One day my father called at the farm to take me fishing. He must have borrowed some tackle from someone and I distinctly remember that it was a blistering hot day. We fished near the lighthouse and there are two things I still clearly remember from that day. The first is of a large dead fish laid rotting on the beach and it was the foul, fishy smell from it I remember most. The other is the bait that we used. He had obtained worms of some description, from where I do not know, and put them in a condensed milk tin which was not quite empty. I recall gazing into the tin in amazement at all these condensed milk covered worms slithering about in the bottom - was this some secret bait additive to attract the fish? I don't think so. It didn't attract many fish that day and the only one I can recall was the dead one lying on the beach.

I have some other vague memories of my father taking me onto to the base, and in my mind I see pictures of sand-bags, but in what context I don't know. I also recall being in what I now presume was the cook-house, and then being in some building which housed some unknown type of machinery. Here again, above all else it is the smell of oily rags and solvents in this building that remain clear in my mind. Another very distinct memory is one of gun-barrels pointing skywards. However it is not the guns that make this image so memorable, I probably hadn't a clue what they were anyway - it was the sheep. Grass covered the area surrounding the guns and there were lots of these sheep stuck with their heads down munching away. I can only assume that is what they were there for - to keep the grass down.

I recall one day sitting on top of a five-barred gate in a field adjacent

22

to the base, watching the air-men trying to deflate a barrage balloon. They had it on the ground and were all jumping onto it, like a giant bouncy castle, and they were all shouting and laughing and having great fun for my amusement, I probably wished I could have joined in too. How long I actually spent with Mr and Mrs Perry and their family on their farm in South Wales I don't know, but what I do know is that all my memories, limited as they are after more than sixty years, are all of happy times.

Sadly I have no memories of leaving the farm, the tearful goodbyes, or the long journey back to Sheffield. One thing I do know was that Mrs Perry, according to my father, bought me a little overcoat for the journey home so it must have been around autumn time.

During the long years that have passed since those wartime days, my father had often said that one day we should go back to see the Perry family. Unfortunately we never got round to doing it before he passed away and looking back this was always very disappointing. Then about ten years ago, after not being in touch for over fifty years, I decided to see if I could trace the family and the farm where I had stayed. I realised that Mr and Mrs Perry would have probably have passed on by now, but there was a son, Ron, and two daughters, Eileen and Hilda, who probably still lived in the area. The only real information I had to go on was the family name and the area near Newport referred to by my father in later years as Nash point. I tried several lines of inquiry, but to no avail. Then out of the blue one Monday evening I received a telephone call. The voice on the other end was that of a female with a strong Welsh accent. She asked:

'During the war did you stay on a farm in Wales?'

After a moment to get over the shock and emotion:

'Yes' I replied.

'Well, I'm Sheila wife of Ron, whose parents' farm it was you stayed on' she continued.

They had suddenly, out of the blue, decided to trace me at the same time as I tried to trace them - an unbelievable coincidence after more than fifty years. My wife and I went there for a weekend a few weeks later and stayed with Ron and Sheila. We also met Ron's sisters, Eileen and Hilda. Unfortunately the old farmhouse had been demolished and the land compulsorily purchased many years before. The presence of a power station now obliterated any hope of walking in my childhood footsteps but the old lighthouse on the fore-shore (where I once went fishing with my father), is still there. We are still in regular contact and have recently learned that the power station has been demolished and the site is now a wildlife sanctuary - a more fitting end.

Now back in Sheffield after my convalescence in Wales, my next memories are of starting school and I remember very clearly the morning my mother took me to St Barnabas's Infants' School on Alderson Road (now a bed salesroom). The class room had a large open fire and there was an extra-large high fire-guard surrounding it. There were children bustling about, and a few grown-ups, then mother left and I was on my own - once again the tears started to flow. Blimey! I must have been a mardy little perisher, but once again I soon got into the daily routine of school life.

Three distinct images emerge from this early period of school life. The first was of going to what must have been a harvest festival service in St Barnabas's church, the first church that I ever remember entering, and hearing the hymn 'All things Bright and Beautiful' springs into my mind. The second was going into another air-raid shelter, which was built in the corner of the playground, without being bribed with sweets. The third was of making friends for the first time, two children in particular who lived opposite the school.

A short uneventful period followed and school life continued in the usual pattern before fate struck once again. A lump had developed on the right side of my neck. Here we go again, more Doctor's bills for my mother to find. So it's off to the doctors once again; the Doctors Gorrard and Rodgers (I remember them well) who had their surgery at the bottom of St Mary's Road on Club Garden Walk. The first diagnosis was nothing too serious and a tin of Kaolin poultice was prescribed:

'That will be twelve and six pence thank you very much' said the doctor - or words to that effect.

At this time many different types of poultices were used to treat all kinds of ailments, from sprains to mysterious lumps etc. The poultice prescribed for me came in a small silver tin and I remember it well. The content of the tin was grey in colour, looked like putty and was to be placed in a saucepan of water and brought to the boil. After heating it was spread on a piece of pink lint and then applied to the neck while it was hot, the hotter the more beneficial according to the doctors instructions. This was considered a cure in those days but it was more like a torture. I remember trembling with fear every time a saucepan was placed on the gas ring. After a while my mother could see this treatment was doing no good whatsoever, so it was back to the doctors. A further diagnosis decided it was now an abscess and needed surgery, the meaning of which thankfully I was quite unaware.

The next image in my mind is of lying on a table surrounded by people in white gowns - I was now in the operating theatre of the Royal Hospital. Suddenly a cloth of some description was placed over my face and this was when the fighting began - the kicking, the screaming and the flaying of arms. It soon became apparent why there were so many people round the table. Pinned down and unable to move, a strange smell filtered into my nostrils; the fight was now over and I drifted into oblivion. I awoke to find myself the proud owner of an ugly looking scar on the right-hand side of the neck which to this day looks as though the person responable for the sewing was more accustomed to sewing mail-bags. Unfortunately, after all that the problem had still not been solved and I was now diagnosed as having a TB gland, a common complaint at the time due to drinking un-pasteurised milk - that is milk straight from the cow.

I now found myself in a large Victorian house type building, standing in its own grounds, the access being down a drive on Farm Road, just off Queen's Road. The building is long since demolished and was eventually replaced with a bowling alley and an ice skating rink (Silver Blades)[2]. My mother and I were ushered into a room. There was an examination table up against a wall and a man and a woman, dressed in white coats, were sat at a desk. I was invited by the man to lie on the table, but already having experienced what happens when you lie on a table once before, I declined his offer. Then the woman produced a white paper bag containing sweets which she said would be mine - or words to that effect if I would lay on the table facing the wall. Either she or the sweets must have been very persuasive because I now found myself lying on the table facing the said wall. Suddenly I felt a sharp pain in the back of the neck, my mother had got me by the legs whilst the other two had have got my head and shoulders in a strangle hold. Within minutes the pain ceased and I was released. I learned later in life that they had inserted a syringe into my neck and had drawn off whatever it was that was causing the problem. I still have the dent in the back of my neck to this day. Thank god medical practices have improved.

Daily doses of malt, orange juice and cod liver oil were now prescribed, plus I was sent for a few sessions of sun-ray treatment. This took place in the same building where about half a dozen of us were sat in a semi circle around a large lamp emitting a strange purple glow - similar to today's sun-beds. We sat there stripped to the waist for about half an hour per session, wearing what I can only describe as welders goggles to protect the eyes. How many sessions I had of this I don't now recall, but by the end of it I had once again made a full recovery and I resumed my place back at school.

These first few years of my young life must have been very traumatic for my parents, especially my mother who not only had to cope with my problems on her own, but had to do so with a war raging on around her. Fortunately this was to be the last of my illnesses for a very long time it would be many years before I saw a doctor again - in fact the next time was when I was eighteen years old.

2 Now the Grosvenor Casino and Rollerblading Rink.

I was invited by Her Majesty's Government to attend a building on Ecclesall Road above *Hartleys* potted-meat factory, to be examined by not one, but a team of doctors. If, in their opinion I was fit enough (that meant being able to see), had all the appropriate limbs and being of a sound mind, I would be given the choice of either going to jail or serving two years in the army. I decided the latter was the best option. It was called National Service, something every eighteen year old male, in the country had to do. The only exception being miners working down the pit, or young men on apprenticeships which could get deferred till they were twenty one. I could have been deferred, but opted to go in earlier and get it over with. But that was all in the future, the important thing now was to get my young life back on track.

Chapter Two

GOT ANY GUM CHUM?

It was now all about getting out and about and acquainting myself with the surrounding area again, as well as meeting some of the other children who lived there; something I had not been able to do in the recent past. My school life had also resumed and I rejoined the class at St Barnabas's where I made a few friends, but only as school pals.

The majority of the new friends I met were children from the neighbourhood where I lived, and over the next ten years we all grew up together, sharing many childhood experiences and adventures. At that time they didn't attend the same school as me, they went to Duchess Road School, that was until it was hit by a German bomb and then they were transferred to a Roman Catholic school, St Marie's on Edmond Road. Later on we were all given a choice of the junior school we would like to attend. Most of my friends had opted for Pomona Street, but my mother wanted me to go to Sharrow Lane School like my sister. It took a lot of persuading on my part to get her to change her mind, but she finally agreed.

Pomona Street County School, as it was then known, was just off Ecclesall Road and this was to be the school that would educate us all until we were fifteen years old and ready to start work. The war at this time was still raging on, but to us kids it was now just a part of everyday life, made just a little more interesting when the Yanks came to town. After a few recent expeditions up the bomb-damaged town we were now beginning to become quite street wise, in the nicest possible way.

One of our favourite ploys at the time was to go up The Moor and hang about round the old Victoria Memorial at Moorhead, looking for American servicemen. There were usually a few knocking about sitting on the plinth under Queen Victoria's statue. They used to frequent the pubs around Moorhead, particularly the *Barleycorn* on Cambridge Street, well noted at the time as the haunt of prostitutes; even we knew that - don't ask me how at our age. But like I said earlier, we were now becoming very street wise.

Another of their favourites was *Nell's Bar* next door to the Hippodrome picture house, a cinema which was to feature prominently in our later life. The yanks, as everybody called them, were usually very generous to us kids; we'd approach them and utter those popular words of the day:

'Got any gum chum?'

27

More often than not a stick of chewing gum, or some other delicacy, would appear from a pocket in their uniform and handed over much to our delight. We never pestered them like street-urchins; even at that tender age we knew how far to go, politely appreciating everything they gave us. Then suddenly, as if by magic, they all disappeared leaving us, and no doubt the girls in the Barleycorn, all a little disappointed.

We had a fad at that same period of collecting empty discarded cigarette packets that were strewn about the town centre. There were dozens and dozens of different brands of cigarettes from all over the world. Some of the packets had quite attractive colours and designs on them, making them most collectable. We used to do swaps among ourselves and were quite proud of our collections. I used to keep mine in a paper carrier bag hidden in the attic until one day my mother found them:

'What the bloody hell are these?' She asked.

'My cigarette packets' I replied proudly.

'Well you can bloody get rid of them' she exploded, 'You don't know who's had them or where they've been.'

I wouldn't have minded but I'd only got about forty! It was time for a new hiding place.

The Moor and the surrounding area at this particular time was one of our familiar haunts which we explored regularly. It was badly damaged during the German blitz in December 1940 and many of its old pre-war shops were either bomb-damaged or flattened entirely leaving us kids plenty of ruins to explore.

The most dangerous structures had been levelled to the ground, but some of the old cellars still remained intact. I remember one instance of us entering one of these cellars, on a lane which ran parallel to The Moor, this cellar in turn led into another cellar under *Philips* furniture shop, a shop that had been damaged during the blitz but was still standing and by that time still partially trading. It was obviously dark down there so we each screwed up some old corrugated cardboard we'd found and set it alight to make torches (where the matches came from I haven't a clue). As we walked through into the second cellar we spotted what looked like bodies lying among the rubbish which covered the floor. In the panic to get out some of the torches, still burning, were dropped as we fled like scared rabbits. Passing the scene later on our way back home, we saw to our amazement a fire-engine standing outside the building. Nonchalantly strolling past we noticed a pile of tailor's dummies smouldering away by the entrance to the cellars.

Another favourite playground, also on The Moor, was the basement

The first night of the Sheffield Blitz, December 12, 1940

Looking up The Moor after the Blitz – the remains of Atkinsons is on the left

29

Blitzed out Sheffield

A shot down German bomber became the star
attraction as it was exhibited in Barkers Pool

remains of the bombed out old pre-war *Atkinsons* store (the new one at the bottom of the Moor is built on the original site). The large basement area of the old shop was about eight feet below pavement level, open to the elements, and rain water a few inches deep had gathered in the bottom turning it into a gigantic paddling pool. We spent many happy hours there; sailing lumps of wood, throwing bricks into it and generally larking about as only little boys will do - and always finishing up with wet feet.   By now we had formed our own gang of pals, the Hereford Street Gang, not a gang of hooligans - more like a gang straight out of a 'Just William' book. We were full of adventure with a little mischief thrown in. With most of our fathers away in the forces pocket money was an unheard-of commodity; in fact to be quite honest pocket money was a phrase that never even entered our heads. If we wanted a few coppers we had to earn them ourselves, and being a bit street wise we had our methods, all legal of course.

One sure fire way was selling buckets of sticks for the fire. Everyone had an open fire in those days so there were lots of potential customers, and with all the bomb-damaged derelict buildings around the area at our disposal, old timber was plentiful. At 3d a bucketfull we were soon in business.

Another scheme was collecting used jam jars. The *Maypole* grocery store at the bottom of The Moor paid us a penny for a small 1lb jar and tuppence for a large 2lb one. This was one money making idea though that was not very profitable owing to the fact that jam jars were a bit scarce.

One good idea to make a few pence we actually got from a wartime poster, one of the many wartime posters splashed on walls about town at that time. It read 'Save Salvage' or words to that effect, so that's exactly what we did. Armed with a sack apiece (we had all acquired these from somewhere) we'd set off up The Moor and adjacent streets, entering into all the shop's back-yards, at least all those that were still standing and open for business, and filling the sacks with any old paper, cardboard and rags we could lay our hands on. By now we knew The Moor and the surrounding areas like the back of your proverbial hand; all the nooks and crannies had already been well scrutinised by us so we knew the best places to search.

One of the favourite areas was the Arcade at Moorhead. This was a covered walkway between The Moor and Union Street with small shops on both sides. Access to the back-yards was down a passage way between the shops and this was the entrance to a salvage collector's dream-world. Sacks would be filled up in no time at all, especially from the rear of *Hodgkinsons Camera Shop*, a haven for paper and cardboard. Then it was off to the salvage yard to weigh in. *Marsdens* rag-yard, as we called it, was located at the Fitzwilliam Street end of Button Lane which ran from Moorhead to Fitzwilliam Street. The entrance was through a pair of lattice gates, so with sacks slung over the shoulder we would make our way down to the old metal weighing scales in the middle of the yard to be confronted by an old woman dressed like a figure from a Charles Dickens novel. Her steel-grey hair was tied in a bun, she wore a long black dress which touched the floor as she walked and the dress was covered with a long black pinafore. She was the person who did the weighing and the paying. She would take the first sack, throw it on to the scales, and do a bit of adjusting with the weights on the sliding scale to get the weight correct:

'That will be tuppence' She'd say, 'Go and empty it in there' pointing to a brick building across the yard.

Everybody got the same amount, even if at times you had collected more than anybody else, it was still tuppence. This got our devious little minds thinking:

'Was the old bugger conning us?'

We decided to test her. The next time we went in one of the lads wrapped a house brick in with his salvage. He craftily tried to place the sack gently on the scales himself but before he managed it she took it off him and dumped it on the metal platform herself. There was a dull clang as the brick hit the metal scales. She scowled at him, pulled the sack off the scales and emptied the contents on the ground. The brick fell out hitting her on the foot and there she was hobbling about as she chased him out of the yard. He was banned for life. Talk about re-cycling - we were doing it sixty odd years ago.

There were other ways we had of making a few coppers, but more about them later. On another salvaging trip up The Moor we got the shock of our lives. We had started at the bottom searching all the back-yards of the shops, but as we approached Moorhead we could not believe what came into view. Parked in front of us on a piece of waste land at the end of Button Lane, and by the side of the Women's Land Army Recruitment office, stood a massive great Lancaster bomber:

'How the hell has that got there? It definitely weren't there a couple of days ago.'

We hurried across the road to get a better view of this fantastic aircraft parked in our back-yard. It was probably there on some fund raising exercise. On another piece of waste ground opposite, by the side of *Freeman, Hardy and Willis* shoe shop, stood another aircraft. This one was much smaller, probably a fighter, but apart from its size the only other thing I recall about this aircraft was part of it was painted yellow. Could it have been a captured Messerschmitt which I believe had a yellow nose-cone.

Another popular playground of ours, both during the war and after, and also on our doorstep, was St Mary's churchyard on Bramall Lane. We spent endless hours in there playing all kinds of games amongst the Victorian grave stones which incidentally were no obstruction because the majority were all flat. The churchyard was a lot larger in those days and surrounded all the way round by a six foot high stone wall with a row of tall trees, Elm or Sycamores, running down the Bramall Lane side. The churchyard was entered through two large wrought iron gates which were also situated on Bramall Lane between the trees. A wide tarmac drive led down from the main entrance to the church-porch but we mainly entered by climbing over the wall on St Mary's Road.

Part of the wall and the pavement slabs on the Bramall Lane side of the churchyard were pitted with holes and, this was due to strafing courtesy of the Luftwaffe during the blitz. All have disappeared long ago due to road widening - all in the name of progress. It was in the confines of these walls, using coats or jumpers as goalposts, that furious games of football took place. In the cricket season we played robust games of cricket with an old tennis ball, and bat and stumps designed and made by us out of some old wood. Then there was the chasing game that we called 'tiggy' which is unheard-of today, also every little boy's favourite, climbing trees - and not forgetting of course the mass skipping sessions. For this a long rope was obtained with someone on each end turning, and everybody else skipping en-mass. All these games involved vigorous exercise, no wonder we were all thin; no junk-food to gorge on, in fact hardly any food at all, but we certainly got plenty of exercise to keep us fit and healthy.

One thing we didn't do was get bored and we always found something to do. Sometimes we did things we really shouldn't have been doing and such activities often took us into forbidden territory - in the church itself, or rather the tower of the church. During the war and for quite a few years afterwards the church was not used, All the windows were boarded up and all the doors were permanently locked, all except one, and surprise-surprise, who was it that discovered this little snippet of information - the Hereford Street Mob of course. With a little bit of squeezing, we found that we could ease our skinny little bodies through the gaps in the wrought iron gates that barred the entrance to the church itself, and gain access to the entrance of the church foyer. On the left was a smaller door, closed, but as we soon found out - not locked. This door was the access to a stone spiral-staircase leading eventually to the roof of the tower. Filled with a sense of adventure, but little other sense, we nervously started to climb the stone stairs. Owing to the light from the open door below, we could see part of the way up, but the higher we climbed the darker it became. We cautiously continued climbing, in single file, ever upwards in the dark until after a few more turns shafts of light started to illuminate the staircase from above. A couple more turns brought us to a doorway leading into what we could now see was the belfry about halfway up the tower, and the wooden lattice windows on each side of the building was the reason for the sudden influx of daylight. I don't recall how many bells there were, I just remember peering through a small hatchway into the vast loft space above the main area of the church. Pigeons were flying in all directions as we disturbed them, causing clouds of dust to shimmer through the shafts of light penetrating the gloom. Passing through another door opening in the belfry, the staircase continued up, so once more we started to climb - eventually coming out onto the roof of the tower. What a view. Not a pretty view however, houses, factories and smoking chimneys - but quite mesmerising considering that the highest we had ever been was the top deck of a tram-car. I remember we were very careful not to put our heads above the parapet just in case we were spotted, by a policeman for instance (they walked the streets in those days - there were no panda cars).

We visited the tower a few times after that, but one occasion stands out more than the rest. It was just after the end of the war. We had just entered the belfry when suddenly the organ in the church started playing at full volume - we were down that staircase and out of the church in double quick time. We then casually walked round to the rear of the church, as though butter wouldn't melt in our mouths, and came across a now opened side door. The haunting strains of the organ being played so professionally filtered through the doorway and we all crowded round the door and stood in awe at a man sat at the massive organ, playing away just like Reginald Dixon. The front of the organ was lit up and the man suddenly turned round, spotted us, smiled, and carried on playing. On seeing that he was friendly we all timidly entered the dimly lit church and sat down on the dusty pews - not a word being spoken. What an odd sight we must have looked - a group of scruffy kids sitting in a dusty church lit only by the shafts of sunlight beaming in through holes in the boarded up windows. It was a church that had not seen a congregation for years and there we were being entertained by a maestro on the organ. If only someone had had a camera.

One day we heard from some source or other that an American B17 bomber had crashed in Endcliffe Park, so it was on the tram and up to the park for a bit of souvenir hunting. The crash site was at the back of the café in the woods beyond the river which we crossed via the stepping stones (these are still there incidentally). We climbed up the incline to the actual crash site but there was absolutely nothing left. Apart from a few scars on the trees there was no indication a crash had ever occurred; the salvage teams had done an excellent job. The ground all around the site had been thoroughly raked over and although we

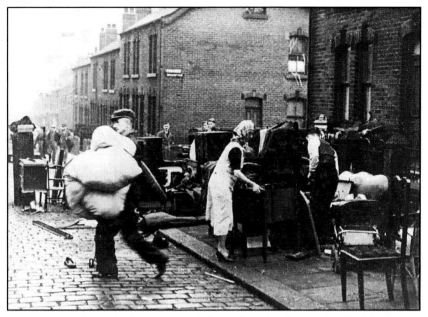

Furniture being rescued from bombed out Sheffield
houses in the aftermath of the Blitz

The water filled basement (right) was all that was left of
Atkinsons after the Blitz – we regularly went home with wet
feet after playing here

searched around for a while for any souvenirs, we found absolutely nothing. There is now a memorial stone on the site and a memorial service is held there every February attended by both American and RAF personnel. After the service there is also a march past by veterans from the British Legion led by a local pipe-band which is quite moving. I always try to attend when possible as I feel I am part of it in a small way; I don't know why, probably because it happened in our area and in my era. Maybe it is because we had stood on the spot where a few days earlier the entire crew had perished trying to avoid children playing in the park; a park where we ourselves had played in on numerous occasions.

It was a warm summer's evening probably sometime in 1944. We were messing about in St Mary's churchyard as usual when from over the other side of the wall, in Bramall Lane, came the sound of engines. Peering over the wall we saw about a dozen soldiers all wearing red berets and climbing off motor bikes outside the *Queen Adelaide* pub. This caused great excitement and we were soon over the wall in double quick time. We had never seen so many soldiers on our patch before, especially soldiers on motor bikes:

'What were they doing here? What did they want?' were questions we asked ourselves as we scrambled over the wall. We soon found out the reason - obviously they'd come for a pint.

The *Queen Adelaide* was a lively and popular pub at that time. It had a concert room with a small stage (which would be graced with our presence in the not too distant future). Music from the piano together with cigarette smoke and the aroma of beer used to pour through the open windows on a summer's evening. I remember passing this pub on many occasions and hearing the chatter and laughter of people enjoying themselves - even in those uncertain times. It was to this venue that the lads from the Paras had called for refreshment and it wasn't long before we were amongst them admiring their bikes. In later years I found out that they had probably come from the Parachute Regiment's depot at Hardwick Hall in Derbyshire. One or two of them suddenly decided to give us kids a ride on their bikes; and so, sat on the handle bars and leaning back into their chests (there was no pillion seat) they took us on a ride down St Mary's Road, across Shoreham Street and then on down to Queens Road to the bottom of Granville Road. They then turned round and biked back up to the *Queen Adelaide* pub. I remember all of us being absolutely thrilled to bits. It was a night of thrills, laughter and excitement courtesy of the 'Red Devils'.

The reader may wonder about any other traffic on the roads. The plain answer is that there was hardly any at all - especially after teatime. In later years I often wonderered where these lads had finished up; were any of them killed in some heroic action? I don't remember the exact date when this event occurred, but what I do recall is that it was a warm night probably during the early summer of 1944. On D-Day the 6th June 1944, the airborne division dropped into Normandy in northern France. In September of that same year they dropped into Holland (operation market garden) and many men perished in these two operations. Some of the lads who provided us with so much pleasure on that memorable night may well have been involved in either of these two operations. Hopefully they all made it back home safely.

The long drawn-out war was now nearing its end and suddenly at the beginning of May nineteen forty five all the guns fell silent. It was over - well nearly over as there was still Japan to see to. All the celebrations followed and the adults, or most of them, started immediately. Our VE (Victory in Europe) party was held a couple weeks later and took place in the *Hereford Arms* pub organised by the women of the neighbourhood. The food they provided was truly amazing considering that it was in short supply and still on ration. There were sandwiches with various fillings, homemade buns, lemon and jam tarts made by my mother, even trifle was on offer - and of course lemonade probably provided by the pub landlord and landlady. It was a truly memorable feast of goodies, the likes we had never seen before; let's face it we'd had nothing to celebrate before. The war had suddenly come to an end, no more playing war-games, no more hanging around town looking for suspicious looking German spies. No more sirens, deserted air-raid shelters; whatever are we going to do now. Little did we know at the time that a whole new world was out there waiting to be explored, and it didn't take us long to get started.

Chapter Three

PEACE-TIME

One of the most striking differences after the war had ended was when the lights came back on - by lights I am referring to street lighting. We had spent the last six years living in total darkness at night, especially in winter time. So to see all the streets illuminated was something of a novelty to us. Most of the streets still had old Victorian gas-lamps. During the war years we'd used them for shinning up, or to use as a swing by throwing a rope over one of the arms. Now they were important everyday items to be respected - or else! They also provided someone with a job and we used to call him the lamp-man. He had a small ladder and his job was to walk the streets, stopping at each gas lamp and placing the ladder on one of the arms. He'd climb up, clean the glass inside and out, then wind up the clockwork mechanism that turned on and turned off the light at the appropriate times. If I remember correctly the only roads that had electric lighting were the tram and bus routes, and even some of those were gas lit. The bus routes were mostly on the back roads however.

Looking through the bedroom window at night with all the streets lit up by gas light was like a wonderland after six years of darkness. It also meant we could stay out longer playing on the streets, I remember all the chasing games plus other activities, which have now disappeared into oblivion. The exception to this was the fifteen minutes between 18.45 and 17.00 daily when we all went indoors without fail. This was the time when the latest episode of *Dick Barton Special Agent* was on the wireless and we very rarely missed that.

One of the first old-time traditions we restored was Guy Fawkes Day, better known as Bonfire Night. Bearing in mind we had never even seen a bonfire, apart from those that Hitler created, or had ever made a guy; it didn't take us long to learn but from what source, or who told us, I haven't a clue - but learn we did, and fast. The first thing we learnt was that there was a copper or two to be earned from this bonfire lark, so putting our salvaging skills to good use we set about making our first Guy.

A pair of men's trousers, and a jacket, were acquired from somewhere or other and stuffed solid with paper and cardboard; we then set about making the head. This was made out of a white linen flour bag, (flour was sold in linen bags in those days and also made excellent fishing nets), together with a piece of wire and a cane. The head was then stuffed solid and tied off. All three items were then wired together (don't ask were the wire came from but we were al-

It was in the cellar of Philips furniture store (right) that
we accidently started a fire

The Victoria monument at Moorhead - the Yanks used to
sit on the plinth at the base and shout 'got an gum chum'?

ways quite resourceful) and the artwork on the head started. This is where we altered the legend slightly. Instead of a nondescript Guy we fashioned a Hitler-Guy complete with black hair almost over the eye, and the notorious little black moustache. This we carried on to The Moor and placed it in a very prominent position with a sign round the neck saying 'Penny for the Guy'. It proved to be a nice little earner for a few days prior to burning and it certainly beat salvaging financially.

The size of the bonfires in those early days after the end of the war was something else. Ours was erected on a piece of waste land between a cobblers shop and *Tim's Barbers* at the bottom of Bramall Lane. This land was adjacent to the River Porter, part of which can still be seen from the car park in front of *Staples*. The collecting of bonfire wood started about a month before and with so many bombed and derelict buildings in the surrounding area, timber was easy to come by. Well, easy to come by is not quite true. If today's health and safety jobsworths had seen what we got up to in our search for bonfire wood they would have had a heart-attack. But by 5th November not only did we have a bonfire stacked more than ten feet tall, we had enough reserve timber to keep it going for a week. At the height of the burning, it was that hot nobody could get within twenty foot of it; roasted potatoes were definitely out of the question, at least until the fire had subsided a little. Talk about global warming!

After that first fantastic fire, those in future years had to be built round the corner on a more open piece of waste ground in Hermitage Street. The reason being that, adjacent to the old site, there was a small workshop that put handles on cutlery and the material used was highly inflammable. The owner feared that sparks from the fire might set his premises ablaze.

Over the following years we had some tremendous bonfires, but as the old bombed out buildings were pulled down and flattened bonfire material became more difficult to accumulate. Then along came a new source. New modern furniture soon became widely available and people started to upgrade their homes. Hire purchase was introduced and new bedroom furniture, dining suites and modern three-piece suites were now in the price-range of most working class families. So it was out with the old and in with the new, with the old going on the bonfire. One year I remember three three-piece suites plus wardrobes all going up in flames. That was of course only after we had searched in the nooks and crannies of the settees and chairs to see if there were any coins.

Fireworks were a bit limited in the early days after the war. Penny-bangers were popular, as were Catherine Wheels and Jumping Jacks, especially when thrown among a group of people (boys will be boys) but rockets were rare. Potatoes were thrown into the embers around the edge of the fire, but the problem was retrieving them before they burnt to a cinder. The fire was so hot that a length of timber was used to scoop them out, usually without much success.

Looking back now, what amazes me is how popular Bonfire Nights were. There were bonfires all over the place; explosions going off and the air being filled with unhealthy smoke fumes for days. We spent many happy hours playing on that piece of spare land at the bottom of Bramall Lane. We kept homing pigeons, and also rabbits in hutches that we had made ourselves from orange boxes. The pigeons and rabbits we bought for a few pence from the pet shed in the old rag-and-tag market at the bottom of Dixon Lane. We caught trout from the adjacent River Porter which after a heavy down-pour of rain had been washed downstream from Whitley Woods via Endcliffe Park. One day we lit torches and made our way through the tunnel - coming out of the other side in Mary Street. Over the years we spent hours playing in that rat-infested river with no ill-effects whatsoever. Again, part of the river and the tunnel can still be seen from the car park in front of *Staples* stationery shop at the bottom of The Moor - but alas, that is all that remains.

Whitsuntide was always very special in our young lives. We took part in the religious open-air services (the 'Whit-sings' as they were called) that took place in the local parks which were always popular and well attended, and also the 'Star Walk'' which took place on Whit-Monday. But these were not the reasons why this was so special – the real reason was that Whitsuntide was the only time of the year when we got a new set of clothes, but only providing our parents had the money and the clothing coupons.

The money problem was often eased for most families by acquiring a Provident cheque which was accepted by most clothing shops; re-payment being spread over a period of time. *Blanchards* outfitters opposite the Infirmary Hospital on Infirmary Road was the shop I was dragged to for my new clothes. I'd stand there in the middle of the shop like a tailor's dummy while my mother draped various articles of clothing over me to see if they fitted. I would finish up with a shirt, socks, short trousers, (we were about eleven before we got long trousers) and sports jacket, all two sizes too big and with those immortal words ringing in my ears:

'You'll grow into them.'

'Yes when I'm about bloody thirty.'

Dempseys on Duke Street was the popular shop for our shoes, plimsolls and, on one occasion, a pair of bloody clogs. Come Whit Sunday, after a good scrub, we'd be dressed up in our new clothes and allowed outside for a couple of hours to show off, but before we got through the door further instructions would be issued:

'No climbing or playing football in them new shoes, and keep away from that river' in this case, the River Porter at the bottom of Bramhall Lane

Walking round the block like Little Lord Fauntleroy in your new clothes, with your hair all stuck down and parted made recognising your friends a problem. We'd walk past one another wondering:

'Who the bloody hell's that?'

Part of this new tradition was to knock on a neighbour's door, and when it was answered you would ask the question:

'Do you like my new clothes?'

Their response should have been 'Yes', and to then place a penny in your top pocket. Unfortunately some people hadn't heard of this new tradition, or had conveniently forgotten, and their response was usually a single word:

'Lovely!'

Then shut the door in your face.

Charming!

Chapter Four

MUMMERING

Christmas time was just as special to us kids in the 1940s as it is to kids nowadays - probably even more so. The big difference, of course, were the presents we found in our Christmas stockings which weren't quite like the presents expected by some of today's kids. We didn't get things that needed batteries, or had to be plugged into the mains, but the thrill of looking to see what Father Christmas had left was just as exciting.

Some of the popular presents of the day were boxes of paints, painting books, jigsaws and maybe an apple and an orange depending on availability. We didn't get much, nor did we expect much; we were quite content because we all, more or less, got similar presents. Later on, after the end of the war, Christmas took on a whole new meaning to us - it was 'mummering time'. How we, as ten-year old kids, who had spent the previous six years living in a total blackout knew what it was to go out mummering at Christmas and New Years Eve is a complete mystery to me even now. A few years ago, out of curiosity, I checked in a dictionary to see if the word mummering was there, and found much to my surprise that it was. The definition of mummering was: 'to mask', 'to sport in a mask or disguise' or 'a masker', and that is exactly what we did - especially on New Years Eve. These days kids go carolling, we went 'mummering' - singing carols with a difference.

We targeted not only the local houses but also the pubs, at least those with friendly landlords. The other big difference was, we all had black faces (masks or disguises) and this was achieved by rubbing soot, from the back of the fire, onto our faces. Sometimes lard was applied first, and then the soot, creating a real shiny black 'Al Jolson' finish. Where the hell we got this from I haven't a clue. I don't remember anyone ever telling us about it and we certainly never saw anybody else do it. The mystery remains.

Of the two days, Christmas Eve and New Years Eve, the latter was the most favoured and was the most profitable because letting in the New Year in peoples homes after midnight found the occupants in a merry and generous mood. You may ask: 'What were your parents doing, allowing you to stay out till that time of night?' The simple answers is, without going into detail again, times then were a lot different than in today's Britain.

Christmas Eve was always a good time for mummering and we usually finished before ten o'clock, but New Years Eve was something special. The gang would meet outside the *Bricklayers Arms* in Hereford Street at around seven o'clock, all blacked up like a gospel choir (try getting away with this nowadays), with Ostermilk tins at the ready. I'd better explain. Ostermilk was a free powdered baby food of the day and it came in a round tin about six inches tall and about four inches in diameter. The empty tins were easy to come by and were then used by us in various ways. On this particular occasion, with two holes punched under the rim at the top, and a piece of string threaded through to form a handle - they made ideal collection tins to hold the pennies we hopefully made from our singing. Sticklebacks from fishing trips were also kept in these tins, as were acorns packed in salt collected from the Millhouses and Ecclesall woods in the autumn, which we actually ate believe it or not.

Anyway I digress - back to New Years Eve. We were now ready to start and as I recall, we started carol singing at the houses around the local neighbourhood, but not with a great deal of success because the response generally was:

'Too early!'

It was only when we started visiting the pubs that the evening livened up and we could rattle our tins. Now the marathon pub crawl began. The first call was back to the *Bricklayers Arms* at about eight o'clock; Mr Lake was the landlord then, a nice chap who always let us in to sing a carol or two. The pub wouldn't be too full at that time, and the people who were in were quite generous and appreciative. Next, it was round the corner to the *Chantrey Arms* at the bottom of Bramhall Lane, this was a small pub nestling in amongst the row of terraced houses. I can't actually recall if we were welcome here or not.

The next pub, on the corner of St Marys Road, was *The Norfolk* as I remember it. This always seemed a dingy dark place to me with not much going for it; that pub got only one carol thank you very much. Now the next pub really was a pub, the *Queen Adelaide* which stood at the corner of Bramall Lane and Hermitage Street. Having already referred to this pub earlier, and having explained that we were soon to go on to grace its stage - well this was one of those nights. We were always welcomed here, if not by the landlord then certainly by the customers who would shout to him:

'Let them in you miserable sod.'

So it was into the concert room and onto the stage amidst all the laughter and the jokes. For some in the room it was probably the first time they had seen a gang of kids, all with black faces, mummering and singing carols and they were in for a shock. Before we go any further I would like to mention that the majority of us were choirboys, believe it or not, at St Mary's Church on Matilda Lane. This was a small church used whilst the church on Bramall Lane

We were always refused entry to the Travellers on The Moor so
we helped ourselves to the odd soda siphon from the backyard and
claimed the half-crown deposit from the corner shop

The Pump Tavern on The Moor – another
good mummering pub

The Angel on Button Lane – one of our favourite
mummering pubs

Millets at the bottom of The Moor – the shop
where we bought hiking and camping gear

was closed. Complete with cassock and surplus, we sang at services on a Sunday morning for the princely sum of 3d a week, provided that we turned up for choir practice on a Wednesday night (we'd do anything to earn a crust). So you see, we weren't just pretty black faces - we could also sing a bit. The customers of the *Queen Adelaide* got our full repertoire, much to their delight, and they showed their appreciation as we went round the tables with our collecting tins.

The next pub on our journey was *The Star of Lamont* just a few yards up Hermitage Street from the *Queen Adelaide,* and this was a one carol pub - being a bit quieter than the previous one. It was now that we went back to the top half of Hereford Street heading towards The Moor. There were two pubs here that received our attention and the first was the *Bridge Inn* on the corner of Porter Street. The outside façade of this building was covered in bright yellow vitrolite, a kind of shiny glass-like material that made it stand out on a bright sunny day. The landlord let us in but I don't recall it ever being busy, so this rated one carol only. Higher up on Hereford Street, on the corner of an intersecting lane, was *the Hereford,* a smallish pub with not much atmosphere. However, this pub had hosted our VE Day party so we showed our appreciation.

We now turned right and started to venture up The Moor. It was now action all the way because all the pubs from now on were vibrant, and by this time of night the customers were well-nourished and in a merry mood. The first pub was the *Travellers Rest* but unfortunately this landlord would never let us in - the miserable sod. He always had 'turns' on in the pub but every week the same name appeared on the board outside. The name was 'Loopy Lee', what he did on stage we hadn't a clue but it certainly kept us out. On the odd occasion we used to see this character going in and out of the pub during the day - you couldn't miss him really. He was a small thin person who wore glasses, but the most unusual thing about him was that he wore knee-length trousers. In fact at that period, just after the end of the war, there were a few characters knocking about town. One character wore a RAF great coat and had a pair of welding glasses on his forehead. We used to call him Rommel and he went round town looking in all the litter bins. Another character was nick-named the Duke of Darnall, always immaculately dressed in a pinstripe suit complete with bowler hat and spats. He would suddenly walk into the middle of the road, in the centre of town, and start directing the traffic. Another was Nora, later known as Pond-Street Nora. She walked about town, absorbed in her own world, effing and blinding.

A few yards up from the *Travellers Rest*, but still on The Moor, was the *Pump Tavern,* the original pub which was later pulled down and rebuilt round the corner. It was another good old-fashioned pub, well patronised and run by a lady known to the locals as 'Aunty Pump'. She would always allow us in to do our party-piece and so this establishment always received our full range of carols. Once again the clientele showed their appreciation as the collection tins went round.

The next pub was a bit of a mystery really, situated just before the Victoria monument and the old toilets at Moorhead. This was the *Devonshire Arms*, a single storey prefabricated building that had been erected on a piece of waste ground. On this site the old *Redgates* shop had originally stood until it was bombed by the Germans during the Sheffield Blitz. The mystery was - why build a temporary pub in an area which was already surrounded by many pubs. Memories of this pub are very scant other than its unusual position, set back from the road and on a piece of waste ground.

We knew exactly where we stood regarding entry into the next pub - no chance! Just round the corner at Moorhead was *The Grapes* which was a large one-roomed pub whose entrance was through a circular revolving door. It was this very door that got us barred. During the rest of the year the novelty of this door used to attract us like a magnet and whenever we were passing we could not resist piling in, pushing it round, and then dashing off before the landlord could get to us from behind the bar. But we would still try to gain access at Christmas. We'd pile into the door, shove it round and enter the pub, hoping he'd not recognise us with blackened faces - but he always did. I can see him now. As soon as he spotted us he'd come to the edge of the bar, arm outstretched and with a firm finger pointing in our direction:

'Out!' He would bellow.

It was back into the door, a quick shove, then out into the street. I think we only did it to annoy him, the miserable sod.

The next few pubs where a bit hit and miss really and some years we got inside to sing a carol or two, other years there were no-go areas. These were *The Nelson,* opposite *The Grapes* at Moorhead, then across the road up Cambridge Street was *Nell's Bar* and *The Barleycorn* (no chance here), then on to Cross Burgess Street and *The Athol*, but only occasionally were we allowed in there.

Like all good things, we kept the best till last and the next pub is the one that I will always remember. It stood at the end of Button Lane at Moorhead and was called *The Angel.* To enter it you first went under an arch into a little courtyard, then through a door on the left. It was a typical town pub of the day, lively and with a lot of atmosphere, and I remember on one occasion the lot of us standing in the middle of the room, singing a few carols and then getting a tremendous reception. Our choirboy training had paid off and the financial rewards weren't bad either; one man dropping a half crown into my tin, which was a lot of money to us kids. Did he mean to do this or did he mistake it for a penny whilst being Brahms and Liszt - I will never know.

It was now time to head back down to Hereford Street, do a few more houses and then have the big share out. Oh yes, I nearly forgot; there was one more tradition that we always did and this took place after 12 o'clock on New Year's Eve. This was what we called 'letting the new year in'. After singing a carol or two outside someone's house, preferably one with the sound of jollity coming from within, we'd knock on the door and nine times out of ten would be invited inside to let the new year in. The first one over the threshold tradition-ally had to have black hair; this was crucial and once inside that same person would be handed the poker and had to stoke the fire up (every house had an open fire and a poker in those days). This was another ancient tradition and it was supposed to bring good-luck to the occupants of the household for the coming year. Another tradition that is unfortunately long gone, there being few open fires and very few pokers.

Winter time also had other childhood benefits - the snow. It was always guaranteed and usually lasted for more than a few days, sometimes weeks. This was sledging time. We all had a sledge of some description in the cellar which was homemade and usually built using timber from bombed out buildings. The sledge irons were scrounged from the many engineering works in the area. Nor-folk Park was one of our favourite places for sledging, down a steep hill, a great sledge run, in the direction of Farm Road. Another run was down Sunny Bank, a road just off William Street which itself is off Ecclesall Road by the side of *The Star* cinema. This was a steep traffic-free side road and made an excellent sledging run, the only danger was being able to stop at the bottom before shoot-ing straight across William Street in front of the odd vehicle.

Chapter Five

SCHOOL DAYS

Life at school was becoming much more interesting. We were now at an age when the subjects we were being taught were being absorbed more easily. Woodwork was one of the new lessons we boys were introduced to, for the girls it was cookery lessons - two practical subjects handy for the future. The first requirement for woodwork class was a white woodwork apron (so you could see the blood); mine was made for me by my mother who thought I was six feet tall.

'You'll grow into it' she said once again as I stood there with six inch of it trailing on the floor.

For the first few months we had to walk up to Hunters Bar School for the lesson as we had no wood-working facilities at our school at that time; or should I say marched there - because the teacher thought he was still in the army. Later on two prefabricated buildings were erected in front of our football pitch; a woodwork block for the boys and a cookery block for the girls. I distinctly remember that first lesson at Hunters Bar learning about the different tools and their uses, before he turned us loose on an unsuspecting piece of timber. The first task, the teacher informed us, was to plane the timber, or wood as we preferred to call it, face side using a wooden plane which seemed about four foot long and required two horses to pull it.

'Next, plane one edge making sure it is square with the aid of your set square' he said. This was easier said than done.

One of the lads could never get this task quite right and every piece of wood the teacher gave him was soon reduced to a pile of shavings. After reducing half the Brazilian rain forest to shavings the teacher clearly thought:

'This bugger's taking the piss - I'll have to sort him out.'

So he gave him a piece of timber the size of a giant redwood and told him:

'Plane that down.'

He spent every lesson in the weeks that followed planing this lump of wood down to a pile of shavings.

We had some really excellent old school teachers, both men and women, who could illuminate the subject lesson being taught to really make it interesting. They were fair but strict as anybody who stepped out of line soon found out; discipline was paramount and the cane was dished out quite regularly. I was a recipient on more than one occasion. Anyone who says caning didn't hurt is kidding; you only told your mates it didn't hurt after standing in front of the class with a straight face, trying to convince them it wasn't hurting, not bloody many it weren't!

One of our teachers was Mr Clinton who took us for various subjects and he had this habit of throwing the blackboard eraser about the class room. While standing with his back to the class, writing something on the black board, he'd hear someone in the background whispering. In a flash he'd spin round, pick up the blackboard eraser, and throw it in the general direction of the noise - everybody would duck down in unison. The eraser was actually a piece of felt on a hardwood base, and pretty heavy. I never saw it actually hit anyone, but if it had they would certainly have known about it.

He was also very handy with the cane and we all remembered it well. It was only small but the effort he put in, bringing it down onto someone's hand, made the veins in his neck stand out. He really meant to hurt, the sadistic sod. During the Olympic Games held in London in 1948, Mr Clinton was one of the swimming officials and once a week he would march us up to Glossop Road baths for swimming lessons. It was through these lessons that I and lots of other boys under his tuition learnt to swim, going on to get all of our distance certificates and finally the intermediate and bronze medallions for life saving. Oh and not once did he have to use his cane as we all of us enjoyed it so much.

Another one of those good old school teachers was Mr Ward, a disciplinarian who knew how to get the best out of a pupil. Three of the subjects he taught were geography, history and spelling and with his commentary he made these usually dull subjects, as far has most pupils are concerned, most interesting. It was probably the prize money at the end of the lesson that had something to do with it - especially the geography and spelling lessons. Before each lesson started he would write a list of questions about the subject he was teaching on the back of the blackboard. Ten minutes before the end he would spin the blackboard round for us to write down the answers and the person with the most correct answers was rewarded with a three penny bit. It may not sound much nowadays, but we could buy a lot with three pence in those days. Other than that it also gave us an extra incentive to listen and learn. His motivation was to get the class interested in the subject being taught, and although his methods were probably a bit unorthodox, they certainly worked - however hard it was on his pocket.

Mr Murray was our music teacher. He also ran the school football and cricket teams and was another teacher that used incentives to get results. However you didn't always get what he promised. I recall my last Christmas at school when I was playing centre forward for the school football team on our own cinder pitch at the rear of the school. We were playing St Silas's, a local rival, in what was like a derby - it was also the day of our school Christmas party. The score as I remember it was 1-1 when suddenly, in the space of about three or four minutes, I scored two quick goals, followed shortly after by another. Mr Murray then shouted from the touch line:

'For every goal you score, you can have two extra buns at the party.'

With a little bit of luck I finished up scoring enough goals for all the team to have two extra buns each, but the reward on this occasion proved not to be forthcoming. He was also an excellent pianist and would illustrate his lessons on classical music with a burst on the piano, making the subject that little more interesting. Then towards the end of the lesson he would play a medley of popular songs of the day, all jumbled up and with some of the notes altered to disguise them. The person who wrote down the most correct titles was rewarded with a sixpence, and the winners were always girls!

I remember an occasion when he took us to Sheffield City Hall to listen to a concert by the Halle Orchestra. The hall was full of school children from schools all across the city and we were seated behind the orchestra at the rear of the stage near the statues of two lions. Through his teaching we could identify all the instruments being played and recognise each of the pieces of music being performed. What appeared at first to be another dull day, turned out really interesting and enjoyable - in fact I can still recall some of those classical pieces almost sixty years on.

Looking back on those school days at Pomona Street School, they were happy times; the lessons were pretty basic by today's standards but we left school at fifteen able to read, write, spell and add-up. History lessons were about British history, giving us something to feel proud of, unlike the so called politically correct curriculum of today. Physical training and team games were encouraged and played a healthy part in our school life. All our written work was done with pen and ink (biros came on the market during our final year) and everyone took it in turn to be an ink monitor, whose job it was to make sure the ink wells on all the desks had a full ink pot in them every morning. When recalling this to my four year old grandson one day, he asked:

'Did you write with quills granddad?'

The final year pupils also took it in turns to be milk monitors, responsible for the distribution of the free daily half-pint bottle of milk to all the pupils in the school. There was a perk in this chore an extra bottle of milk.

Considering we were an inner-city school, we were very lucky to have our own football pitch; the surface unfortunately was red shale - not grass. But this was no detriment and robust games of football took place on this rugged surface. Swimming was a year round sport we all enjoyed immensely - mostly at Glossop Road baths. Schools at that time provided, on request, what were called 'bath cards' and these cards had a page of perforated tickets, similar to a page of stamps, that entitled the holder entry into the baths at half-price which was about three pence in old money. We regularly took advantage of this concession during the year and come summer time it was outdoors bathing, or anywhere that held water, that received our attention - providing it was not too dangerous. Millhouses Park was one of our regular venues where we would dam the River Sheaf with rocks until it was deep enough to swim in for a few yards. We also swam in the boating lake until the park keeper chased us off. But our most favourite place of all, when we could afford it, was the fantastic open-air pool but unfortunately we couldn't use our bath-tickets here. The pool in Millhouses Park was something else; it was twice as long and twice as wide as Glossop Road baths and I recall one memorable visit there.

The day was perfect, warm and sunny with a cloudless sky and it was only ten in the morning. It had been a good week, gradually getting hotter day by day. The tar between the cobbles in the street had started to bubble up again. We sometimes made marbles with it, rolling it in our fingers until we got the same shape and size as a marble, then trying to get the tar off our fingers before our parents saw it.

The only place to be on a day like this was Millhouses open-air swimming pool, so with our trunks rolled up in our towels we made our way up Cumberland Street (now Cumberland Way), to catch the tram. The tram-stop was at the bottom of The Moor, outside *Bullivants* green grocery shop. We always looked round the back of the shop to see if there was any 'spec' (bruised) fruit, slightly damaged but quite edible. Out of luck today, probably old Jim from the Salvation Army Hostel opposite (the old one - not the new one) had beaten us to it. In a while the tram came clanking down The Moor and came to a halt at the stop. We all boarded and shot straight upstairs into the back-bay.

Derrick took up his usual position under the seat – Derrick never paid if he could help it. The rest of us all sat over him with legs dangling to hide him from the conductor.

'Nah then lads' he said when he finally decided to come upstairs for the fares, 'Where're you going, swimming?'

'No Mister, we've been down town pinching towels.'

'Don't be bloody cheeky or I'll have you off't tram. Come on let's have your half-pennies.'

At Millhouses terminus the tram ground to a halt. We all alighted and

Yours truly displaying my prefect's badge, prior to demotion... Note the new American baseball boots. The houses in the background are on St Mary's Road, now St Mary's Gate

On holiday with Graham, sister Joan and mum

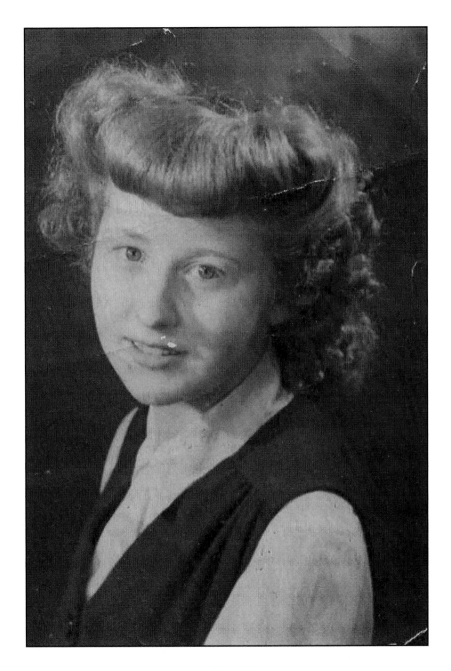

My sister Joan

made our way to the pool pay-box. After paying and collecting the metal basket to put our clothes in, we undressed and handed in the basket in exchange for a numbered disc which you handed in to get your clothes back.

At last we were here. The pool looked magnificent, shimmering in the warm sunlight. It was twice as long and twice as wide as any other baths, and twice as cold as it was unheated. At the north end stood the diving platform, an enormously high structure with three diving levels. To young children it looked as high as Blackpool Tower. THostel opposite (theo simply jump off the top diving board was awesome. We only did it once, that was enough, and I remember the moment like it was yesterday.

But first a swim:

'Last one in's a cissy.'

We all raced to the edge of the pool and dived in. It was like diving into the Arctic Sea, it took your breath away. Two breadths of the pool and then it was back out for a bit of sunbathing. We lay on the grass which surrounded the pool for a while, admiring a stocky blonde-haired man with a barrel-chest diving off the high-board. He did a couple more dives, just to make sure nobody had missed him - then he retired to sunbathe. Nobody was on the diving platform now and there was no one swimming in the deep-end.

'Come on lads it's our turn now' somebody said.

'Go on! I dare you.'

The challenge was to jump in from the top splash, a very daunting challenge to small boys. My heart missed a beat.

'Shall I back out?' I thought. I certainly wasn't keen.

'I can't be a coward though, the others would never let me forget it if I didn't do it.'

We made our way down to the pool-side and to the diving platform. The nearer we got the higher it looked.

'Still time to back out.'

Hesitantly we started to climb the steps to the top. At the first platform I looked down.

'Not too bad, keep going.'

At the second landing I was definitely beginning to wish I was elsewhere, and by the looks on the other's faces - so were they. Someone started to climb to the top, like sheep we followed. The view from the top of the tower was breathtaking. Peering over the safety-rail, it was a long way down to the water. The diving board protruded out from the tower, a bit like walking the plank. One had to walk out into space with no handrail, before diving, or in our case, jumping.

We stood there for a while clutching the safety-rail deciding who was to go first. My turn came and with my heart in my mouth I walked out to the end of the board. Without looking down launched myself into space - a bit like jumping out of an aeroplane over the sea I suppose. The sensation was exhilarating and my stomach came up to join my heart in my mouth. The journey down seemed endless, then with a crack my feet hit the water and I disappeared into the depths (twelve feet deep).

Down and down I went, slowing down as I neared the bottom; then the fight to get back to the surface. With the sensation of the jump, and the impact of the cold water, I was gasping for breath and the journey up to the surface seemed like an age. At long last my head broke water and I gasped in the fresh air before swimming to the side of the pool. We stood there beside the pool elated, as though we'd just won gold in the Olympics, a memory that has lasted over fifty years.

We spent many happy hours in this pool during the long warm summers of our childhood, until some silly persons from the council decided to close it down and turn it into a lido with silly little pools that were neither use nor ornament. That didn't last long and the site has finished up as a derelict piece of land for years, depriving future generations of a once fabulous amenity. I strolled through Millhouses Park one sunny morning this summer. I peered over the railings and the sight that met my eyes was very disturbing. Where the pool used to be was an overgrown tangle of weeds and bushes. What a waste. What a crime[3].

The war had been over for about a year now and new interests were beginning to enter into our lives. Football was one of them. We had always enjoyed a kick-about but now we could see a real professional game courtesy of the boy's entrance (entrance fee 9d) on Bramall Lane, so it was no surprise that I became a lifelong Blades fan. In fact I was football crazy.

I hardly went anywhere without a tennis ball in my pocket and every spare minute I'd be dribbling down the street rounding some imaginary opponent, or kicking the ball at a wall which didn't make me very popular with some of the neighbours. There with one certain person in particular who lived in Mary Lane, a quiet lane with no traffic which ran between Bramall Lane and Hereford Street and was therefore ideal for playing football.

This old dear, who lived in one of the two houses in the lane, had me

---

[3] This section is reproduced from a letter that was originally published in the The Star on 30th December 1999. The site of the old swimming pool and the later Lido at Millhouses have long since been redeveloped. The 'Splash' and 'Fishway' projects have seen the construction of an interactive water-play area as well as a separate water-course, consisting of a series of channels and rock-pools, allowing the river trout and other fish to bypass the weirs on the River Sheaf and to swim upstream. No doubt the author would have welcomed of these improvements.

down in her book as an all-round bleeding nuisance (her words not mine) and the instigator of all the football matches which took place near to her front door (which was true), and she was to wreak her revenge on me later. This sweet caring old dear decided to organise a coach trip to the seaside for all the nice lovely children who lived in the area, all except one that is; no prizes for guessing who that was! When asked by our next door neighbour why I was not included, she replied that all the seats had been taken, which later proved to be a lie. She had her revenge but it didn't bother me, we still carried on playing football.

The majority of our football games were played with a worn-out tennis ball but later on we acquired from somewhere an old full-sized leather match-ball which obviously then called for a change of venue. We would have got some real ear-bashing if we'd started kicking this ball about in front of you-know-who's door. The new venue was a piece of waste land in Hermitage Street where we also had our yearly bonfire. This proper match-ball also attracted more players, sometimes fourteen and fifteen a side and games were played at a frantic pace. Everybody wanted to have a kick at this new ball at the same time; in fact the ball spent more time in the river than in the back of any goal. Being wet made it twice as heavy as it was when it was dry, which was bloody heavy enough. Another problem was, the ball not being new and taking that much stick, that it often got punctured so it spent quite a lot of its time in *Jack Archers Sports Shop*, opposite *Richdales Brewery* on Bramall Lane - constantly being repaired. However, this was only when we could afford the two shillings that it cost to repair it, which included the repair of the punctured bladder, inflating and putting in a new lace.

A few years later at the age of fifteen I got the opportunity to play for Oaks Fold - Sheffield United's nursery team at that time. Quite a few of United's local players graduated to the senior team from this nursery club. Mr Swallow was the team manager at the time and the home ground and training ground were in Concord Park; but with having to travel from one side of the city to the other on two buses, I found it a bit of a pain to get there and missed most of the training sessions. I was informed of the match day details every week by postcard, but shortly before the end of the first season I lost a bit of interest in the game and finally packed it in. This is something I regret to this day because I really think with a bit more effort in attending training sessions, and with more of the enthusiasm I had had when I was younger, I may have progressed further. I really feel that it was one of life's missed opportunities .

Apart from watching the odd football match when we could afford it (9d through the turnstile at the boys' entrance) United's ground received quite a lot of our attention - especially during the cricket season. This was not because of our love for cricket you understand, the real reason was due to another of our money making schemes - collecting empty bottles. The ground at that time was shared with the Yorkshire Cricket Club and during the summer three day county league games were played there. During the football season only three sides of the ground were used, but during the cricket season there was access to all four sides of the ground. The cricket lovers, who were very numerous, sat on cushions on the concrete steps of the terraces surrounding the ground, watching the game. Most of them brought their own refreshments and pop bottles in those days had a deposit of 3d on them. This is where we came in - armed with the sacks we had previously used for our salvaging expeditions during the war. We'd make our way up Bramall Lane and then round the corner in to Cherry Street. It was here we gained access to the ground; over the wall when nobody was about, usually in the late afternoon. It was now that our work began, making our way round the ground in and out of the spectators looking for empty pop bottles. When one was spotted we asked:

'Do you want that bottle mister?'

The usual reply would be:

'No take it away kid.'

It would then disappear into the sack. This would continue all around the ground or till the sack became too heavy to carry. Our exit out of the ground was easier than the entry; the gates would be open for people wanting to leave early and it was then off to the local corner shop to cash-in. The most amazing thing about this money making scheme was that during all the times that this took place we were never challenged once by any of the ground staff. Thinking about it, we may have been doing them a favour - getting rid of something that somebody else would have had to attend do. The only time we were ever challenged was when a policeman saw us attempting to climb over the wall, but before he could get to us we were off down Bramall Lane like a herd of galloping horses. We were all wearing clogs at the time, a cheap form of footwear courtesy of *Dempseys* shoe shop on Duke Street.

Chapter Six

ACROSS THE DERBYSHIRE MOORS

It was during this same period that I first started to develop an interest in the great outdoors. Our wanderings into the countryside so far had been limited to the local parks and adjacent woodlands. There was also the odd walk from the tram terminus at Meadowhead to the tea-gardens at Apperknowle via Coal Aston. This was many years before the building of the Batemoor and Jordanthorpe housing estates when the area was still open countryside.

I had recently joined the Central Lending Library (junior section) which was, and still is, housed in the Graves Art Gallery building at the top of Eyre Street. We spent quite a lot of our time in the art gallery, especially during the winter, browsing and looking at the paintings and other objects on display. This was mainly because it was somewhere to go that was warm and dry.

Amongst my favourite books at the time were the 'Just William' stories, but I generally enjoyed any boys' adventure books like 'Biggles' or books about football. I was particularly taken with the 'Out with Romany' books. These were a series of books all about the countryside - the moors, the woods and fields, and the coasts around Britain. They were filled with descriptions of the flora and fauna, the birds and animals, the butterflies and insects that inhabit these islands. They really stirred-up my childhood imagination and I couldn't wait to get out into this new and fascinating world that I had discovered - far away from the bombs and destruction we had recently witnessed in our everyday lives.

I was about ten or eleven years old when one day I came across a small paper-back book entitled 'Across the Derbyshire Moors' published by the then 'Sheffield Telegraph and Star'. This book described various rambles in Derbyshire together with maps and other relevant information to help the traveller on their way. After a bit of study we found a few of the rambles actually started within walking distance of where we lived, or at least a halfpenny tram-ride away. This book was definitely going to broaden our horizons and we couldn't wait to get started.

It was once again a warm sunny day when early one morning we set off with jam sandwiches and a bottle of water packed in an old ex-army gas mask case bought for just a few pence from *Millets* ex-army stores at the bottom of The Moor. We boarded a Fulwood bound tram at the bottom of The Moor and got off at the terminus at Fulwood Church. After consulting the guide book we started our ramble down Brookhill and after passing the shops on the left we climbed for a mile or so up a country lane until a right-turn took us onto Lodge Moor Road. This eventually brought us to the back of Lodge Moor Isolation Hospital (as it was then known) and I remember us standing there for awhile - looking around at this new landscape. We then took a left-hand turn down a track and crossed a large grassed field to be confronted with the perimeter wire of what looked like a prisoner of war camp, complete with prisoners (apparently) and watch-towers.

At the time we had no real idea what this place really was, or of its existence, but we were intelligent enough even at that tender age to put two and two together. We stood there and looked in amazement at all the wooden huts and all these men behind the wire dressed in an assortment of tunics. Each prisoner had a black diamond shape sewn onto to the back of their jacket. Some of them were walking around whilst others were stood about in groups just talking. We were a bit apprehensive as we approached the wire. We knew that the war was over, but as far as we were concerned they were still the enemy. Nobody told us to move on so we walked casually along the perimeter wire staring at them, more out of curiosity than anything else. Over the previous few years we had obviously heard lots of stories about the Germans but this was the first experience we had had of coming face to face with them. It certainly wouldn't be the last. I can't remember if this part of the ramble was described in the book, I suspect that we had deviated slightly from the route - something we were to do on a regular basis on our future journeys.

Leaving the camp behind us we now joined the main road to Redmires passing the *Three Merry Lads* pub on the right and eventually arriving at Wyming Brook. It was here that we turned right leaving the road behind to begin a steep descent through some scrub and moorland heading towards various dams which we could see in the far distance. After a short while I remember that we stopped for a rest and a jam sandwich, and I looked at the route-map in the book to try to identify the dams that we had observed. These turned out to be the Rivelin dams and so we were on the right track. Suddenly somebody shouted:

'Bloody Germans!'

Looking up there were two German prisoners climbing up towards us on the path not far away. Thinking that they'd escaped we were up on our feet like lightening, stumbling and falling down the hill through very rough terrain - beating a hasty retreat. We never stopped running until we just about reached the dams in a breathless state. I bet those Gerries had a right laugh at our expense. We passed the camp on a few other occasions that same summer during our rambles in the area and we often came across more of them walking in the

At Longshaw
in 1949

Me rambling
somewhere in
Derbyshire

On our wedding day

countryside. We became used to seeing them and got quite brave - walking close by them whenever our paths crossed[4].

Over the road from the dams was a pub outside which was the bus terminus and it was here we caught the bus home. Our first full day in the countryside had been quite a change from the city-life we had been used to; fresh air, birds singing, large open skies, a new and totally different environment altogether - and of course bloody Germans!

'Brilliant, we'll have some more of this.'

The prisoner of war camp is obviously not there anymore but in the woods at the back of the *Sportsman* pub at Lodge Moor the brick foundations of the huts can still be seen in amongst the trees.

After this first jaunt we started to get more ambitious and over the next few years we travelled further afield and explored a large area of the Peak District to the south of Sheffield. One of our favourite rambles started in Endcliffe Park, a halfpenny tram ride from the bottom of The Moor yet again. According to the book the route took us through the park, across Rustlings Road and on through Whiteley Woods to Forge Dam and then up Porter Clough and the Mayfield Valley to Ringinglow. At this point there were two alternative walks and we did both of these on different occasions. The first route involved a turn at the round house leading down onto the old Roman road which we followed to Fox House. In those days the road was broad and pretty level but today it is deeply rutted and unrecognisable from sixty years ago - probably due to the steady stream of Land Rovers. The alternative route from Ringinglow took us along the main road as far as Burbage brook, a left turn to follow the stream down across the moor, onwards around the foot of Carl Wark and then a short stride to Toads Mouth. After a detour through the Longshaw Estate we would finally arrive at the bus terminus at *Fox House Inn* - and then home.

These rambles into the countryside of Derbyshire were now taking place on a regular basis during the summer months. We usually referred to our trusty guide book and eventually we tried out all the different routes that were to be found within in its pages. Sometimes however we would deviate from the set route to create our own walks that were more to our convenience. In time they began to take place over greater distances and I remember one typical walk

---

[4] Lodge Moor POW camp began as an Army training camp during WW1. It was converted into a POW camp towards end of the war and one of its most famous inmates was Admiral Karl Doenitz who later became one of Hitler's deputies and actually succeeded him briefly after the latter's suicide in the Berlin bunker in 1945. The camp was re-opened in 1941 and by the summer of 1944 the Nissen huts had become overcrowded and many of the prisoners were living in tents. Most of the prisoners were actually Italians and because they were considered low-risk were given special privileges denied to the Germans. The prisoners encountered by the author in the nearby woods were almost certainly Italians who were working at local farms and were allowed to move freely. The majority of the prisoners were repatriated at the end of the war, but many who were classified as dangerous Nazis were kept in detention for much longer and the camp didn't finally close until 1947.

that also started at the tram terminus at Fulwood Church. For various reasons this trek is still very clear in my mind, one being that it was an absolutely gorgeous day once again - did the sun always shine? Other reasons also spring to mind; the new scenery that was now opening-up in front of our eyes and a few memorable things that happened along the way.

After leaving the tram terminus we followed the usual route, passing the shops and then on up to Lodge Moor. Once again we skirted the prisoner of war camp until we joined the main road and walked as far as Wyming Brook where the road came to an abrupt halt by the side of Redmires Reservoir. I can't recall what year this was but there were still prisoners in the camp so it was probably 1945 or 1946. Whatever year it was we must have had a very good summer because the reservoir was almost empty and I remember looking across the mud-baked floor of the dam towards a small patch of distant water shimmering in the sunlight. We now turned right and started to ascend a steep narrow path, another old Roman road which today is now many times wider after sixty years of hiker's boots trudging along it. At Stanage Pole we rested a while for a bite to eat and to admire the surrounding views across the moor.

It was at this point we decided to ignore the map-route and cut across the virgin moorland to Stanage Edge in the distance. The moor was quite swampy in places, there were no paths or tracks to guide us and so we made our own path as best we could. During our journey across the moor, we disturbed lots of the Red Grouse hiding amongst the heather and I can still recall the whirring of their wings as they took off - flying swift and low above the heather with a high-pitched clucking noise. This was a sound that made a great impression on me at the time - a sound I've never heard again since those far-off days.

After a short while we arrived on the top of what according to the map was Stanage Edge, but the cliff face at this point was pretty steep and during the process of trying to find a way down we came across a cave. We learned later that it was called 'Robin Hoods Cave' and that the notorious Sheffield criminal Charlie Peace had used it as a bolt hole many years ago while on the run from justice. Whether this piece of folklore has any substance I honestly don't know.

We larked about in the cave for a while and eventually found a way down to the base of the cliff, but we were now descending a steep hill - half running and half stumbling through waist high ferns towards a narrow lane at the bottom. On reaching the lane we were now confronted with a big problem. We had deviated so much from the original route that we were now lost. The village of Hathersage had been our original destination so we took a guess at the general direction and followed the lane down a hill not knowing where we were going and, if I remember right, not being all that bothered on such a gorgeous

65

day. We continued along the lane and it eventually started to go uphill skirting a high stone wall. A few hundred yards or so further on and we came to a green-painted door built into the wall (I distinctly remember it was green) and when someone tried the handle - surprisingly it opened. We gazed through and saw that it opened onto parkland with a narrow tarmac road running away into the distance towards where we thought we wanted to be. We guessed it was private property, even though there were no signs to inform us, but as we could see no buildings or any people - we decided to enter and take our chances. If anybody challenged us we'd just plead ignorant. As it happened nobody did challenge us and we just nonchalantly strolled through and came out nearly in the centre of Hathersage. We learned sometime later that these were the grounds of Brookfield Manor.

After buying some refreshments or other at a small shop in the village, probably an ice cream or a lolly, we walked along the Grindleford road and eventually arrived at Leadmill Bridge where it crossed the River Derwent. We peered over the parapet at the river below and because the sparkling water looked very inviting on such a hot sunny day - we decided to have a swim. We could see that there were some steps which formed the weir and these led down to a pool where it looked safe to swim. It looked like an ideal spot to enter the water so it was off with our clothes and:

'Last one in's a cissy'.

I gently slid into the water and I remember that it was absolutely freezing. I thought Millhouses open-air pool was cold, but the River Derwent was something else and we all swam downstream to where it became shallow and then swam back again and got out. We had no towels to dry ourselves so we just had to dry out in the sun which we did after shivering for about half an hour. The next time we swam in this pool we were better prepared.

After we had recovered and were feeling refreshed we continued our journey following the River Derwent through the woods and meadows to Grindleford. At one point I recall that we rested on the river bank flicking pieces of rolled up bread to the waiting river trout hanging about in the current. I also remember a pair of dippers that were jumping from rock to rock and then suddenly disappearing under the water to re-appear seconds later further downstream. From Grindleford we followed the main road up towards Fox House and half way up the hill we climbed over a stile on the right-hand side of the road where a path led us on through the Longshaw Estate to the bus terminus at Fox House. It was then home once again. Over the next few years we got to know this part of the Peak District like the backs of our hands. We made many similar journeys but we had great fun varying the routes, especially the starting and finishing points, which we were able to do comfortably with the cost of tram and bus fares being counted in pennies.

Another occasion that really sticks in my memory was a jaunt we did one cold winter. This was in the winter of 1947 which was really severe with plenty of snow falling. Outside our house there was a covering of about nine inches and this was nearly in the centre of town. After the initial snow-fall the weather turned icy-cold causing all the snow to freeze and to hang about for weeks. Sometime during this period an article appeared in 'The Star' asking for volunteer ramblers to carry bundles of hay up to the sheep stranded on the moors above Fox House. The pick-up point for the hay was the *Dore Moor Inn* because this was as far as the buses could get, and from there to Fox House the road was completely blocked with high drifts of snow. We were full of the spirit of adventure, and with childish excitement at the sight of all this snow - we decided to go and help. We had no anoraks or parkas in those days so I guess we just donned as many layers of clothing that we could find. One article I do remember wearing was my head-gear. We all had ex RAF pilot's leather flying helmets, purchased once again from *Millets* ex-army store at the bottom of The Moor for the price of about one shilling.

After getting off the bus at the *Dore Moor Inn* we walked over to a chap who was distributing the hay. I can't remember exactly what happened at this juncture but I definitely remember walking along the road towards Fox House with a comfortable amount of hay on my back. The tarmac road as I recall, or large sections of it, were still visible for some of the way but large stretches, especially where the snow had drifted across it were a little difficult to negotiate. Once again, as on all our walks, the sun was shining from a clear blue sky but this time it was a winter sun with a searing cold wind blowing. Despite this we kept going and eventually reached our intended destination - in fact we even went a little further and finished up at Toads Mouth where we scattered the hay on the snow by the side of the road. The snow in this area was quite deep in places - too deep and dangerous for us to venture too far onto the moor. How long this journey took us I haven't a clue but at that age time wasn't an issue to us, what I do know is that we got there and we got back and enjoyed the day and the experience.

One of the most amazing things about all the walking we did is that we didn't wear walking boots, or even shoes; all we wore on our feet were black plimsolls, apart from our winter excursions of course. These would have been the very same plimsolls we'd probably worn all summer during all our other leisure pursuits and if a hole appeared in the sole a piece of cardboard was stuffed inside to cover it. Later on brown American baseball boots came onto the market, with a much thicker sole and lasting a lot longer, even despite the hammer that we subjected them to playing football, climbing and all the other activities that boys of our age got up to.

It was when we were aged about eleven or twelve that we joined the St Mary's Scout Troop. We had already graced the St Mary's Cub Pack with our presence, and also the St Mary's Church Choir so now it was the turn of the scout pack. The scout-master was Ron Armitage and the hut that we used for meetings was just round the corner of our street at the bottom of Matilda Lane - close to the little church where we used to sound our vocal chords. Although money was tight we still managed somehow to acquire some semblance of a uniform - all except for the Canadian Mountie-style hat that was popular in those days as this proved to be beyond our means. We really enjoyed those scouting days, learning how to tie knots, woodcraft, experiencing that sense of achievement when gaining a badge - but most of all staying out all night camping in the countryside.

After that first scout camp we were hooked and wanted more of this new activity, but the trouble was that the scouts only went to camp a couple of times a year and our sights were set a lot higher than that. There was only one thing for it, we would have to get our own basic equipment - a tent, a set of cooking utensils, a canvas water bucket and then make our own arrangements. Funnily enough all this equipment came relatively easily. One of the lads exchanged his clapped out air-rifle for an old two man Bukta ridge tent which we turned, with a little squeezing, into a four or even a five-man ridge-tent. The cooking utensils - a set of cheap three-in-one tin saucepans (whose lids made up into frying pans) were acquired from *Millets* after a whip-round - so we were now ready for the off.

The question was when and where to go, but the very first thing was to inform our parents of what we were up to and get their permission. Because we had already been camping with the scouts permission came relatively easily - but then again attitudes about this kind of thing were entirely different from today. So it was that with all our equipment - the tent, ground sheet (an ex-army gas cape) and ex-army blankets etc, we boarded the old Booth and Fisher bus, which stopped just round the corner in Sylvester Street, and set out for Ford Bottom.

We got off the bus at the *Bridge Inn* pub and made our way up Geer Lane, on past the lake on the left and eventually coming to an abrupt end in a farmyard. From here we turned right up a rough track to reach the top of a slight incline where from then on the path suddenly descended steeply down to a stream on the edge of a wood. This was great - and an ideal place to camp.

There was a decent piece of grass for the tent, plenty of old wood for the fire and there was running water - couldn't be better. We soon had the tent erected and after a scout around in the woods we collected enough wood to get a decent fire going. I don't recall exactly what we ate; beans and roasted potatoes would have probably figured somewhere on the menu, but we always drank cocoa or plain water. That first night in our own tent was a riot - the laughter, the tomfoolery, the unfamiliar sounds of the wildlife out in the darkness and all the jostling for a comfortable position within the confines of such a small area. Finally, one by one, we dropped off to sleep in the early hours of the morning.

The next morning after a quick wash in the stream, we re-lit the fire and had a quick brew of cocoa and a bite of something to eat before doing a bit of exploring in the surrounding woodland. The afternoon was spent taking down the tent, collecting our belongings and tidying up around the campsite - all an integral part of our scout training. With regard to any rubbish, especially used tins, the operative words in true scouting fashion were:

'Burn, bash and bury.'

It was then back to the *Bridge Inn* and the bus home.

Thanks to our Scout training we had now added a new dimension to our rambles into the countryside and it was something that we repeated over many weekends during the following months. We visited lots of different locations in the Peak District - pitching our tent in fields, woodland, on moorland and never once being asked to move on. One incident that I do recall happened much later on when we had probably turned thirteen and were starting to grow up a little. We were camping close to the village of Abney near Hathersage when one evening someone had the bright idea of taking the canvas water bucket down to the local pub to see if we could get it filled up with beer. The cost of beer at that time was quite cheap, probably nine or ten old pence a pint, so after a whip-round we clubbed together enough money for four pints. We all strolled down to the *Plough Inn* which is a pub by the River Derwent close to Leadmill Bridge. Obviously there was no chance of us being served, but sat on the wall at the back of the pub were a couple of young men enjoying a pint in the warm evening sunshine. We approached and asked them if they would do us the necessary favour which they agreed to do. Off they went and a few minutes later they re-appeared through the back door of the pub each carrying a pint glass in both hands which were promptly emptied into our canvas water bucket. We thanked them and it was then back up the hill to the campsite where we sat round the camp fire and had a good old sing song with not a cup of cocoa in sight. This, I hasten to add, was just a one off - a young teenage prank and it was probably one of the first signs that we were definitely beginning to grow up.

Chapter Seven

FURTHER HORIZONS

At fourteen years old I got a job as a paper-boy delivering newspapers mornings and evenings before and after school for a newsagents shop in Hereford Street. The pay was ten shillings a week, plus any tips that might be forthcoming, and I collected the money every Friday night. There was one lady I remember well who always tipped me a three-penny bit every Friday without fail. Believe it or not her name was Mrs Mopp. I don't know if this was her real name but that's what we kids always used to call her for years. She was the local spiritualist and her premises were up a flight of stone steps just down the lane from the paper shop, next door to the chip shop. The place used to give me the creeps every time I went in because it was a long gloomy narrow room running the full length of the building. During the week I would open the entrance door and put the paper on a chair, but on a Friday I had to walk the full length of the room to collect her paper money for the week. It was then that she would hand me her tip and I would do almost anything for a three-penny bit. Actually she was a decent old soul and she was certainly well patronised by many folk who obviously believed in that sort of thing.

Like the majority of the lads I was brought up with, none of us had ever had a bike, certainly not a two wheeler, but things were about to change. New cycles were now becoming more widely available. One shop in particular caught our eye - *Wigfalls* on London Road. The shop was filled with them and we would often been seen inside, browsing and casting an eye on some particular model - hoping one day to get our bums on one. They also had this new-fangled way of paying called Hire Purchase. Now not being daft when it came to wheeling and dealing with money, it didn't take us long to realise that this scheme could be the solution to our transport problems. All we had to do now was convince our parents what a brilliant idea it was and get them to put their name on a piece of paper. This was more easily said than done. My parents were very much against Hire Purchase, especially for something that was quite unnecessary like a bike, and it was only after a lot of pleading and grovelling, and a promise to pay for it out of my paper round wages, that my mother persuaded my father to sign the Hire Purchase agreement.

I was full of excitement and I couldn't wait for my father to get home from work on that sunny Friday afternoon. We walked up to *Wigfalls* together and chose the one bike that was most affordable, priced eighteen pounds, and within half an hour I was the proud owner of a brand spanking new red 'Wiggies gas-pipe' cycle - as this particular model was known locally. I was elated. It was a drop handle-bar racing model with Sturmey Archer three speed gears; although in order to win any races on it you'd have had to have had legs like Arnold Schwarzenegger. It weighed a ton, hence the nick name 'Wiggies gas-pipe', but I wasn't bothered because I now had wheels and visions of the open road and distant horizons were flashing through my mind. With my father at my side, I walked the bike home from the shop and parked it proudly under the living room window. Later that afternoon, after tea, I went on my first run. I'd already learned to ride on an old bike belonging to a friend and I had bags of confidence. I remember it like yesterday; up Bramall Lane, across Queens Road then on up Richards Road to Gleadless Road - finally arriving at Gleadless Town End. It was brilliant and I was not even out of breath considering that it was all uphill. I then carried on past the RAF camp at Norton and then down to Four-lane Ends at Meadowhead (as it was then called).

'Boy this is fantastic, such a distance in such a short time.'

I remember feeling very pleased with myself. It was now a right-turn at the Norton Hotel (there was no traffic-island in those days) and on down Meadowhead Hill to Woodseats. Half way down the steepest part of the hill, just opposite the Roman Catholic Church, tragedy struck. I pulled out to overtake a parked vehicle and the front wheel got stuck in the tram lines. The bike wobbled violently and the next minute I'm over the handlebars finishing up in a heap in the road. Luckily the traffic was very sparse in those days even at that time of the day. Nearby was a gang of workmen repairing the road and they rushed over, picked up both me and the bike and took me over to their canvas work-shed. My face and elbow was a bit grazed and bloodied but otherwise I was OK. They got out the first-aid kit and cleaned me up the best they could whilst showing every concern that I was alright, but the only thing I was worried about was my bike. Was my new bike alright? As luck would have it there was very little damage, and I remember feeling very relieved. The old 'Wiggies gas-pipe' was a sturdily-built bike thank goodness. I jumped back on and continued the journey with a bloodied face and a thick lip and feeling not a little disappointed.

On arriving home I parked the bike under the living room window and went in. My mother took one look at my face which was now more swollen than ever;

'What the hell have you done to your face?' she shouted.

'I got stuck in the tram lines and fell off' I replied.

'That's it, that's it!' She bawled, 'That bloody bike's going straight back before you kill yourself.'

Of course it never did and that was the one and only accident I ever had during all the miles I ever travelled on that bike. After that incident the bike and me were inseparable and I would have taken it to bed if I could have got it up the attic stairs.

A few of the other lads had now acquired new bikes also, so our attention now turned from hiking and camping to cycling and camping. Having wheels now extended our boundaries yet further and to pastures new and in the summer we could now have a run out to somewhere or other after tea. Our first bike-rides as a group took us into Derbyshire once again, mainly at weekends, and Matlock was a popular run. This was a twenty five mile each way trip up through Holmesfield and on to Owler Bar, sometimes stopping off at the Clarion hut there for a cup of tea and to gaze in envy at some of the better class of racing bikes that were usually propped up outside. The 'George Dawes' the 'Carltons' and the 'Claude Butlers' were all top quality light-weight racing bikes of the day. They were well beyond our pockets and we could only dream of ever owning one - but we were more than happy with what we had.

From Owler Bar it was nearly all free-wheeling down the hill into Baslow and then on through Chatsworth, the home of the Dukes of Devonshire. On some occasions we would break the journey and linger in the park a while, have a walk round the gardens or a stroll by the River Derwent. Sometimes we just simply lay on the grass in the sun amongst the sheep - drinking in the tranquillity and the beauty of the scenery. From here it was on to Rowsley and then on to Matlock, a place which at that time was a very popular destination for cyclists. At weekends especially it was crowded with cyclists, far outnumbering cars in those days. Unfortunately it is the other way round now. Our final destination would be Matlock Bath where, after a rest and refreshment, we would make our way home. The return leg was in fact the worst part of the trip. The long haul up Baslow Hill, from Baslow to Owler Bar, was gruelling and anyone who got off the bike during this uphill section got some stick from the others. Derbyshire in that era was a haven for cyclists, very little traffic, nice scenery, challenging hills and all within easy reach. There were a couple of Clarion huts, one at Owler Bar and the other near the *Dore Moor Inn* on the Fox House road where you could meet friends and fellow cyclists and purchase light refreshments. Alas both are no longer there.

Our attentions from then on turned from Derbyshire to the flat lands of Lincolnshire, to outings that were longer and took us further afield. These were to be weekend long excursions and involved camping out on the Saturday night. Our bikes were fitted with saddle-bags which contained all the bare essentials required for a weekend long trip, tied on top of that was a rolled up ex-army blanket. We took it in turns to carry the tent which was rolled up and tied with two ropes so that our arms could be slipped through, allowing it to be carried on the back like a rucksack. We were really loaded down and I remember vividly the very first trip that we did, struggling up the old Fence Hill to Swallownest, onwards through Aston and North Anston and then past the golf course at Lindrick and so to Worksop. We passed directly through the town centre, because there was no bypass in those days, and then carried on to Clumber Park where in amongst the trees bordering the road we could see the army Nissen huts where ammunition had been stored during the war. These were demolished not many years later.

From Clumber Park we crossed the old A641 on to what was then the A57 Lincoln road, now a dual carriageway (the A1M). At that time it was just a normal two lane road and we were only about three mile down this road when it suddenly started to rain. As luck would have it there was a barn by the road on the right-hand side opposite a small wood and it was here we decided to stop and shelter for a while. We pushed the bikes through an opening in the hedge and entered the barn. It faced a large field with its entrance open to the elements, but the other three sides were enclosed and it seemed quite clean and dry. One half of it was taken up with ancient farm machinery but in the other half there was enough room to pitch the tent - so in view of the weather it was here that we decided to spend the night. At the back of the barn was a wooden feeding-trough attached to the timber wall which ran along the full length of the building. It was about two feet wide with a sloping frontage and stood about three feet off the ground. On future trips we all slept in this, head to toe, as it saved bringing the tent.

Next morning we were up bright and early and back on the road, it was a gorgeous morning after the rain and not a vehicle in sight. At one stage we were all riding abreast across the road with no hands on the handlebars, our arms were on one another's shoulders as we laughed and joked our way down the road. Our route now took us to Laneham Ferry where we finished up swimming across the River Trent, right to the far bank and back again as it was such a gorgeous day. Looking back over the years to that particular day, I can't believe how stupid we were; in fact I shudder to think of the consequences of what might have happened as the River Trent is quite treacherous. It is tidal in that area so we must have caught it at a low summer level with the tide completely out. Nonetheless we got away with it and returned home safely after an eventful first weekend.

We made this journey on a number of occasions over the coming

73

months, always staying in the barn and never once being challenged by the owner or anyone else for that matter. Most of all we were enjoying the carefree excitement of being free to travel the open road, and of course not forgetting all the laughs we had. The road is now a dual carriageway and a large part of the woods have been destroyed to make way for the second carriageway - but a small part still remains. That magical barn however, with so many memories, is no longer there and I've passed the spot regularly over the years - never failing to glance at the spot and to remember all those happy times so long ago.

I was fourteen when we went on a bike ride to Cleethorpes, one of the longest journeys that we ever made. There were five of us who set off one bank holiday, following the same route taken by coaches on seaside trips organised by the many working men's clubs in the Sheffield area. After the end of the war, these women and children's outings to the seaside were very popular and for a lot of the kids it was the first time they had ever seen the sea. We had all been on these trips ourselves, with tickets being much sought after. The destination was nearly always Cleethorpes; with an identity label tied to our coats, dinner at the *Dolphin* and half a crowns worth of free rides in 'Wonderland'. Because of this we knew the route blindfold.

The weather as I recall it was dry but cloudy, and therefore good cycling weather. We made fair progress during the day passing through Maltby and Bawtry before crossing the River Trent at Gainsborough - then on to Caenby Corner. This part of the journey had been uneventful, stopping just a few times for a rest and refreshments at various villages along the way. Considering the weight we were carrying we were doing quite well time-wise and we had reasonable expectations of making Cleethorpes before teatime, but as we turned onto a road signposted to Caistor it stated to rain. It absolutely pelted it down so we took shelter in an old farm building by the side of the road. The sky went black and there was thunder and lightning for about forty minutes - then suddenly the sun came out and we were in a different world.

There was steam rising from the rain-drenched road as we continued on our way, invigorated by the rest and the warm sunshine, but the chances of us making our destination in time were diminishing fast. On reaching the village of Laceby we decided to find somewhere to camp for the night and eventually we found an agreeable area of grass by the river close to the road where we pitched the tent. Later we rode into the village and found a chip shop were we had some off the best chips and fish I'd ever tasted, well they would be wouldn't they - that was the first proper meal we'd had all day.

That night five of us squeezed ourselves into a two man tent where sleep came easily after all that exercise. The following morning we were all up

Camping at Laceby on our cycle trip to Cleethorpes – the old two man
'Bukta' tent regularly slept five of us

Me on the lane where we regularly played football

bright and early, and after a wash in the river, we decided that as we were not all that far from Cleethorpes we would have breakfast when we arrived. So it was back in the saddle and on the road. It was another sunny morning when we rode into the yard of the *Dolphin Hotel* in Cleethorpes for breakfast and I remember that we were not alone. The tables were filled up with cyclists, and racing bikes of all descriptions were propped up all over the yard. After breakfast we spent the rest of the day wandering along the sea front. We had a walk around 'Wonderland', larked about on the sands, paddled in the sea and had an ice cream etc. By teatime however, I think we'd had enough of Cleethorpes so we decided to cycle back to our previous nights campsite at Laceby and another chip supper. Next morning we were once again up early and after packing our gear we were on the road for the long journey home. We were in the saddle all that day, apart from occasional rest-stops for a little nourishment, and arrived back home in time for tea. It was quite a memorable three day trip.

I remember one Sunday when, for whatever reasons, nobody wanted to go for a run so I decided to go out on my own. I rode to the River Trent at Dunham Bridge following the usual route, then on the way back I stopped beside an orchard at the top of the hill at Markham Moor. The apples on the trees were very inviting, so as there was nobody about I climbed the gate and walked in. After a few steps there was an almighty bang when I walked into some kind of trip-wire device and set off an alarm. I was over that gate and on the bike like lightning and I didn't stop until reaching Clumber Park.

The warm memory of these outings; the rambling, the camping and the cycling trips have remained with me for nearly sixty years. The laughs we had, the mischievous boyhood pranks, the delight of being in the countryside, or being out on the open road, was a sheer joy. In a way I consider that we were very lucky with all these events having taken place in an era so different from the Britain of nowadays. Traffic was only a fraction of the volume of today and young children could generally go anywhere in complete safety, in fact I can't recall a single time when my parents said:

'No you can't go camping' or, 'No you can't go all that way on your bike.'

It wasn't because they were bad parents, or that they didn't care for our safety; the simple fact is that it was a much safer Britain in those days. What has gone wrong?

Our schooldays were now nearing an end (we left school at fifteen in those days) and we were all growing up rapidly. We had all attained a fairly good standard of education, learning to read and enjoying books from an early age. We learnt our times-tables parrot-fashion (if only you could pass a school now and hear the sound of children's voices repeating their times-tables out loud in harmony). We had a basic knowledge of mathematics, it was essential to be able to spell and we were given a reasonable general knowledge of all the other subjects being taught. We finished our schooling without any of today's popular grades or qualifications (there were no tests at that time) and all the subjects we were taught were those considered necessary for when we started our working life - and to stand us all in good stead. In the final year I was made a prefect, probably because I was good at sport, but it didn't last long. One day the headmaster caught me larking about on the school staircase and taking me into his office he told me that I was supposed to set an example to the younger children. Two strokes of the cane were administered just to make sure I didn't forget. Some teachers have no sense of humour. I was instantly demoted.

After leaving school our excursions into the country side became less frequent, we still used the bikes occasionally but other more adult-like interests were starting to take over. Although we were now all working we still had very little money in our pockets in order to indulge in other interests. The early fifties were the start of the pop-music era and, soon after that, the emergence of the 'Teddy boy' culture. Radio-grams and record players became popular and were becoming generally accessible. Records by the popular artists of the day were a must and American singers like Frankie Lane, Guy Mitchell, Johnny Ray, Nat King Cole together with a few female artists frequently topped the recently formed top twenty. Some British artists followed their lead and their records could be bought in the various music shops that were springing up in the town centre, for instance *Wilson Pecks* on the corner of Leopold Street, and *Cann the music man* on Dixon Lane - these being the two most popular.

It was also around about this time that strange girls started to appear round our neighbourhood - when I say strange I don't mean 'peculiar' strange, I mean strangers to the area. We were obviously brought up around girls who lived in our neighbourhood, together with the girls we knew at school, but these girls were complete strangers to us:

'Why are they hanging about?' we asked ourselves, 'What are they after?'

Being constantly in the company of boys, and doing boyish things for so long, girls were never in the equation; but now that we were older we weren't really complaining.

One evening a group of us were stood around just talking when suddenly one of the girls came up to me and whispered in my ear:

'So-and-so wants to go with you.'

Being a bit naive about these things, I asked her:

'Where does she want to go?' I thought she'd got a bike and wanted to go for a ride with us.

'No, she doesn't want to go anywhere' she informed me, 'And she wants you to be her boyfriend.'

So I was now the proud owner of a girlfriend. I still don't know why, we never went anywhere, we never did anything. In fact a week or so later she chucked me and said I was two timing her, and I hadn't a clue what she was on about. I must have been paying more attention to my bike than I was to her - or something like that. I thought:

'Bugger this. I'll stick to cycling for the time being.'

My first job in the big outside world was as an apprentice motor mechanic at *C. D. Bramhalls* garage on Queens Road, a job I had acquired for myself prior to leaving school. I couldn't wait to get started, in fact I left school on the Friday and started work on the following Monday. My tasks in the garage were naturally the menial jobs that all apprentices were expected to do - cleaning parts stripped from engines in a bath of paraffin, grinding-in by hand the valve-seatings in the engine-block, cleaning plugs in the sand-blasting machine and of course mashing tea and fetching sandwiches. It was an interesting job but very smelly and dirty. Every night I'd go home smelling of paraffin, especially my hair. If someone had stuck a match near me I'd have gone up in a ball of flame.

The trouble was we only had a tin bath at home and that only came out once a week on a Friday night. So during the week I had to walk up to Glossop Road slipper baths where you could get a private bath of hot water for a few pence. My wages at the garage were one pound seven shillings and six pence per week which I received in a brown wage packet each Friday. On arriving home this was handed over to my mother un-opened and she would then give me spending money for the week - that was seven shillings and six pence.

'At last I'm rich!'

I'd been at the garage for about six weeks when an incident occurred that brought an abrupt end to my career as a motor mechanic. Every morning vehicles that weren't being worked upon were driven out and parked down the side of the garage. This particular morning I thought I'd give them a hand. I jumped into a van (*Newburys Carpets* were the owners), started the engine and then slowly reversed it out of the garage - so far so good. The problem arose when I started to drive forward down the side of the garage building. There was a slight incline and as I moved forward the van started to run away with me; in panic I shoved my foot down hard, missed the foot brake and hit the accelerator. The van shot forward at speed, and smashed into the garage wall. The front

Doris and me (right) out for a stroll with friends

Military service in 1955 – I'm far right, stood up

Me (right) with friend Bill Hessey

wing was all crunched-in and the headlight that had originally sat on the top was now dangling - suspended on its wires. Every one heard the bang and came rushing out of the garage. I had never had such a feeling of guilt in my life and the garage manager came up to me;

'What the bloody hell do you think you're doing lad?' He spluttered. I remember saying:

'It just ran away with me.'

'Some bugger ought to run away with you' he replied.

Surprisingly I didn't get the sack and it all died down, that is until a couple of weeks later when I told him I wanted to leave. He had me in his office and gave me the biggest rollicking I had ever had - so ended my short career as a motor mechanic.

I left the garage on the Friday without a job and on the following Monday I went to the Youth Employment Bureau on West Street to see what jobs they had on offer. The clerk who interviewed me had a hand full of cards with a different job offer on each of them:

'Would you like to do this?' He asked.

'No' I replied to his first offer.

'What about this then?'

It was a further 'No.'

After going through about another half dozen job cards he said:

'What about learning to be a joiner then?'

He looked a bit shocked and surprised when I suddenly said:

'Yes I'll try that please.'

That is how easy it was for us to get employment in those days and this was just the job I was looking for. I would be working mainly outdoors, which being an outdoors sort person was great, plus the pay was better than at the garage at thirty nine shillings a week. The company was *H & E Horswood Building Contractors* on Ecclesall Road and after an interview with the boss I commenced work on the following Monday.

Even this job got off to a controversial start. I was working on an alteration job at *Remploy* at Handsworth and enjoying it immensely. In fact I was enjoying it so much that as I worked I was singing all the popular songs of the day; the Frankie Lane and Guy Mitchell tunes and many others. One morning after a few days on the job the site foreman came up to me and said:

'I'm sorry but I'm transferring you to another site, your singing is getting on my father's nerves.'

His father was a bricklayer, way past the age of retirement, and was only on the job because his son was the foreman. I must be the only person sent off a job for singing. He actually did me a favour as it turned out because the new site was a far better place to work. This was the start of fifty years of my working in the trade and I have since been employed by many different companies in the building industry.

With regard to leisure time, Dance halls were the 'in' place at the time, but they were off our radar for one simple reason - we couldn't dance. It was in order to make a good impression on the girls that we decided to learn how to dance, but there was no way we were going to prance around in dancing classes. The only alternative was to get someone to teach us privately, so after a lot of coaxing and persuasion a sister of one of the lads agreed to teach us the 'get you round the dance floor basic steps'. Girls tended to know about these things but we hadn't a clue, so one evening after having tea in their front room we started the dance lessons - much to the amusement of their parents. I can picture the scene now, taking it in turns to try to dance with the one female present - left, right, together, or was it left right chassis - or something like that. In the next session she brought in reinforcements; she had no choice really because her feet had taken so much of a hammering. Eventually with a little help from the two girls, and a Victor Sylvester record, we could glide round their front room creating some semblance of movement and rhythm.

We were now ready to be turned loose on some young unsuspecting females at a dance hall somewhere. *Collinsons Dance Studio* was situated down a narrow lane by the side of St Silas's Church, just off Hanover Street. It was a large Victorian house and it was here that we made our entrance into the world of ballroom dancing, full of enthusiasm and anticipation. What a let-down. We bought our tickets from an elderly lady at the door who looked us up and down with not a little suspicion, and then we entered the ballroom - ballroom? It was more like an over-large doctor's waiting room with chairs all round the edge of the room that David Dickinson would have been proud to have in his antique shop. The music came from what looked like the first radiogram ever invented, with records from the same era - we had been expecting at least a small band of some sort. Still, there were plenty of girls about; not exactly beauty queens but we weren't exactly film stars either. We boys were outnumbered about four to one by the girls and we thought that we would have no problem getting a dance here. We were wrong! We sat there for about an hour, eyeing up our potential victims before plucking up enough courage to go over and ask one of them to dance - when suddenly it's the interval. In this establishment that meant a cup of tea at 3d per cup.

We decided that after the interval we would definitely make an effort to put our newly acquired dancing skills to the test. Another record was put on

83

and they were off once more. Apart from two male and female couples dancing together, all the other couples dancing together were girls. We picked out a couple of likely looking girls who were sat down and approached them:

'Can we have this dance love?'

'No thanks' they replied, 'We're sitting this one out.'

So we rejoined our mates and two minutes later they're gliding round the room together - giggling at us. We sat there deflated and by the time it came to the last waltz we were still sitting there. None of us had a dance all night, but we weren't really that bothered; we'd been to a dance for the first time and it didn't really put us off. However we definitely put a big cross on that place.

For our next session, the following week, we tried the St Silas's Hop as it was known locally. This was held in the church hall just round the corner from *Collinsons* and it was a typical church hall and had that typical atmosphere that went with it. The one thing that did surprise us is that it had a small live band instead of a record player and once again the girls outnumbered the boys. All the boys stood around in little groups like wallflowers watching the girls dancing together, and again we decided to wait till after the interval before making a move. What we were doing really was giving ourselves some time to pluck up courage to ask some bird for a dance, hoping we weren't rejected again. Somebody said:

'Well, we can't stand here all night, who's going first?'

We all looked sheepishly at one another but still nobody volunteered. Anyone would have thought that we were volunteering to go into a cage full of lions - but then two of the lads decided that they were going to show us how it was done. The dance was an 'excuse me' waltz, or so we were informed by the leader of the band, and after a couple of minutes two girls came gliding across the floor towards us. These two lads casually walked onto the dance floor, tapped them on the shoulder and said:

'Excuse me.'

One of them turned round, looked him straight in the face, and said:

'No thanks' before dancing away from him. The shamed look on their faces as they walked back had us all in stitches.

Despite that minor set-back we all eventually managed to have our first taste of dancing that night without any complaints of injured feet.

Girls were now coming well into our equation more often and I suppose it was a natural progression for lads of our age. Two or three girls started to come dancing with us regularly so we now had ready-made dancing partners. By now we had begun a weekly routine that started on a Saturday night with dancing at the Abbeydale Ballroom which was downstairs under the cinema (what a sad sight this once great venue is today - standing there derelict and unused.) It also coincided with the beginning of the 'Teddy Boy' era and many lads were now wearing the latest fashions - full drape suits, string tie with the obligatory crepe-soled shoes (commonly known as brothel creepers). We were a bit more sober, plumping for the semi-drape with a slim Jim tie plus the regulation crepes. Once again we never started dancing till after the interval, but this time we had something a bit stronger than tea inside us - just for that extra bit of Dutch courage.

Just down the road was the *Broadfield Hotel* and it was here that we spent the interval downing the odd pint of 'Black Velvet' (cider and Guinness) all of us under age of course. In those days this was a bit dodgy because the police regularly made a habit of walking into pubs unannounced, usually a sergeant accompanied by a constable on the look-out for under age drinkers or anyone gambling illegally. One Saturday night I recall that we were sat in the *Broadfield Hotel* when the outside door suddenly opened and in walked two massive policemen - but as luck would have it some other drinkers had got their attention first. There was a general panic (police were well respected in those days) and a disorderly rush to the toilets; bodies were wriggling through the toilet window in an effort to get out into the street. So with the interval over it was back to the ballroom feeling supercharged - very much a case of:

'Watch out you girls, we're going to dance you off your feet.'

Another ritual that took place every Sunday night, provided that it wasn't raining, was the weekly visit to the cinema. The venue was *The Star Cinema* on Ecclesall Road for the first house of a twice-nightly showing of whatever happened to be the main feature film. It made no difference what film was showing, because this was the place where most young males and females from around that area congregated on a Sunday evening. After the show it was across the road to *Hartleys* for a glass of sarsparilla - then a slow walk up to Endcliffe Park. Here was the main attraction for the evening, promenading through the park hoping to attract the attention of some likely looking female - and possibly to secure a date. Many a date in this park led to marriage.

On a Monday night it was to the cinema once again, this time the *Hippodrome* on Cambridge Street - admission 10d up in the 'Gods'. One can only speculate why it was called the 'Gods'. Probably because these were the highest seats in the cinema, three storeys up and you were sat nearest to the sky - especially on a summers evening when the roof was slid open. Oh yes! This cinema had a sliding roof all those years ago. There were no proper seats in the 'Gods' - just rows of wide wooden steps with a narrow strip of carpet at the front to sit on. There was no arm or back-rests so the trick was to look for some girls, sit in front of them and gradually inch your way backwards so that your back was nestling between their knees in comfort. Some were obliging, others were not.

This was the era when Hollywood was churning films out by the score, some good, some not so good; and every now and then someone in the audience would shout out some funny comment at the screen to roars of laughter. This would usually provoke the two old men who took the tickets to shine their torches into the audience in an attempt to find the culprit:

'Put that bloody light out' someone would shout, 'I thought the war was over' followed by yet more roars of laughter and the stamping of feet.

Compared to what teenagers of today get up to in their quest for enjoyment and entertainment, I suppose our exploits seem pretty tame by comparison. But one thing that has remained a constant is that it was just as enjoyable being a teenager then as it is now - maybe even more so.

The year was now late nineteen fifty two and my father had just got the job of school caretaker at Maltby Street School in Attercliffe. A house went with the job so the time had arrived to leave Hereford Street together with all its memories. It was the end of an era and a great disappointment to me, but I still went up to the old district occasionally, on the bike for a run into Derbyshire, or sometimes on the tram when we were going dancing, or to the cinema.

It was one Saturday night at the Abbeydale dance that my life took a completely new direction. There was a girl who had been accompanying us to the dance and for a while I'd been trying to pluck up courage to ask her for a date. This particular Saturday night I finally asked her and she said 'yes' much to my relief. I would have felt a right berk if she had said 'no'. It was the start of a four year courtship that ended in our marriage - but only after I had finished my two years National Service in the army.

The official looking brown envelope fell through the letter box early one morning in November 1954. I was just leaving for work and the bold letters OHMS printed on the top were the clue as to what was inside. I'd been eagerly anticipating its arrival for a few weeks but as I stared at it lying on the mat, the enthusiasm of those previous few weeks disappeared. It was replaced with a feeling of nervousness and nausea and picking it up I walked into the kitchen and slit open the envelope. The message was short and to the point - report to R.A.O.C. Hillsea Barracks Portsmouth, and a one-way rail travel-warrant accompanied the letter. My call-up papers had finally arrived and like every other eighteen year old in the country I had been invited, nay ordered, to join her majesty's armed forces for the next two years.

I arrived at work that morning, kind of shell-shocked, and the first person I saw was Albert Clover, boss of the building firm *Clover & Sons Ltd* for whom I was working at the time. I informed him that I had received my call-up papers and he was not at all impressed. The reason being - I was an apprentice joiner and he had wanted me to get my call-up deferred until I was twenty one. However I had already told him that I preferred to go in early and get it over with. Later that night I had to inform my girlfriend Doris. We'd been courting for about eighteen months, and if it turned out that I was to be posted abroad, we could be apart for nearly two years. I recognised that it was a long period for her to wait for me, especially for someone as young as she was. I put no pressure on her to do so, but I must admit if she had called it a day I would have been very upset.

In mid November the day arrived to start my journey into the unknown. I had already said my goodbyes to Doris the night before and I left the house about seven o'clock the next morning. My mother was on the doorstep with tears in her eyes; I think she had been in a similar situation once before when she had had waved her brother Bill goodbye as he went off to fight in the First World War. He died as a result of gas-poisoning.

On the journey down I met up with a couple of Sheffield lads who like me were also going to Portsmouth. One was to share the same postings and experiences as myself for the two years and we remained friends for a few years afterwards. The other lad, after training, was posted to Egypt but returned two years later when we were all de-mobbed and shared the joyous train journey back home to Sheffield and freedom. Arriving at Portsmouth railway station we were met by a seemingly friendly army sergeant:

'All the lads for Hillsea barracks follow me please' he shouted.

It was the 'please' bit that made me a little suspicious and this later proved to be justified. There were quite a few lads who got off the train, mainly from the north and midlands, and with a few also from Scotland. Like sheep being led to the slaughter, we followed the sergeant out of the railway station to three waiting Bedford three-ton army lorries.

'Climb aboard lads and we'll be on our way' he said with a shifty smile.

Fifteen minutes later we were passing through the gates of Hillsea barracks, and it would be a whole month and a big lifestyle change before we passed through those gates again.

After climbing down from the lorries we were all ushered into a spacious single storey building to be welcomed with a speech from the commanding officer. The mood at this time was still friendly and cordial; in fact cups of tea were being served all around. The commanding officer addressed us once again explaining it was now time to take the oath of allegiance to the Queen meaning that we were now subject to army laws and discipline as members of Her Majesty's armed forces. It was from that moment on that all the friendliness from those in charge disappeared completely and from now on it was all about shouting and the bawling out of orders. Everything would now be done at the double. We were ordered out of the building and onto the road, and with some pushing and shoving by the NCO's (non commissioned officers) we were all lined up in columns of three and marched down the road in double quick time. Left-right, left-right. Most of us were hopelessly out of step and the instructors were shouting at the tops of their voices - telling us what a shambolic load of shit we were.

We halted outside a long wooden hut and were ordered inside. There were beds and lockers down each side and we were ordered to pick a bed each and to leave our cases and bags there. Then it was back outside again, in columns of three, to be marched to the barber's shop for the standard regimental haircut. This was the fifties and lots of the lads, including myself, had Tony Curtis haircuts and to watch them being sheared like sheep was heart-breaking. We left the barbers shop knee-deep in hair.

We were then marched to the quartermaster's store to be kitted out and the first thing we were issued with was a kit-bag. This was to keep the rest of your kit in - provided that you could force it all in. Loaded down with all this gear we were once again marched back to the billet where the instructors explained what all the kit was for. The first thing was to get out of our civvies and don army clothing - army underwear, socks, denims etc, and then to parcel up our civvies with the brown paper and string provided. These were then posted back to our families therefore severing all connection with civvy-street - we were now well and truly in the army.

For the next six weeks everything was done at 100 miles per hour; from reveille at six o'clock in the morning until midnight. We were marched up and down the barrack square in columns of three for hours on end until we got every manoeuvre absolutely perfect. This was followed by hours of rifle-drill and arms instruction to the same standard of perfection until finally, after about a month, we were allowed out of camp. Not on our own you understand; but as a supervised party - all dressed up in our brand new uniforms. For our first outing we were taken by army lorry on a tour around Portsmouth dockyards including a visit to Nelson's flagship HMS Victory. And so, apart from the occasional period of leave back home, the next two years of my life were spent in unstinting service to Queen and Country.

That period between 1945 and the early 1950s has always been described as the 'decade of austerity' or the 'lean years', there was none of this and there was very little of that. However there were other things that there was also very little of in those days - there were no muggings, there were no 'druggies' and there was no 'benefit dependency'.

I recently observed two old ladies who were standing at the bus stop commenting on the general state of the country today compared to in their younger days. Suddenly one turned to the other and said:

'I'll tell you what, I'm bloody glad I'm going instead of coming, aren't you?'

The other nodded in full agreement.

ALSO AVAILABLE FROM

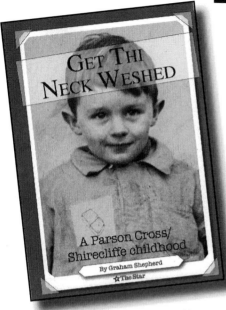

The very bottom of The Moor , on the left you can
just see the Playfair shoe shop where I used to meet
my future wife at the beginning of our courtship